RAISING
A
RAPPER

VENITA MCCOLLUM

First trade printing
Manufactured and Printed in the United States of America

Dedication

To my wonderful Mom and Dad: Thank you for raising me to be the mom that I've become. You taught me to put God, values and morals first.

To the loves of my life, Miles and Nina: Thank you for loving me unconditionally. I gave you life, but you changed my life!

Lastly, for all the young people out there who have doubted their dreams. After reading this, my hope is that you know all things are possible.

Foreword

I was so excited when my mother told me she was writing this book. Not because this is my story, but because the story is really hers. My mother had a dream for me and as I was growing up, she did everything she could to support me in that dream. I had my own dreams, visions and goals, which didn't seem to line up with hers. She saw me in college, pledging a fraternity, and I saw myself rich and famous.

What was great about my mom, though, was that while I know it was tough for her, she allowed me go after my dream. Even when she didn't believe, she gave me space to fly. In the end, my dream really did line up with hers. All she ever wanted for me was to be happy and successful. I've been able to do both, as well as make some of her dreams a reality.

Dreams are made for the young and old. I hope *Raising a Rapper* will inspire children and parents alike to reach for their wildest dreams.

-Miles McCollum AKA "Lil Yachty"

PART ONE
My Story

When you bring children into this world there is no way for you to know what to expect. Then, if you find yourself as a single parent, you have a new set of circumstances that you have to contend with. At that time, all you can do is make sure your child has everything they need, some of what they want, and maybe even a little bit of what they don't need.

Case in point — every time a new iPhone hit the market, I would get a new phone line to get a new phone. The things we do for our kids! You may not want to admit this, but I will — I've done things for my children even when my decisions didn't make good sense. All I can say is that I wanted to do everything for my children.

When my ex and I parted ways, I had a five-year-old and a six-month-old and that little boy and baby girl were my everything; they were my all. I was determined that no matter what was going on between me and their father, I was going to be the best parent I could possibly be to them.

I have to admit, sometimes it was challenging. I cannot tell you how many times I asked myself, "Why do I have to do this by myself? Why do I have to be the responsible one?" There were times when I wanted to say, "I'm gonna just do what I want; I'm going to make it all about me."

However, I knew I wouldn't do that. I wanted to raise two beautiful and great human beings. In order for me to accomplish that, I had to put my children first and myself last. That meant that at all times, I had to do what was best for my children. I was completely committed to that mission.

From the beginning, I knew it was not going to be easy and often times, I wished the time would just speed by. But this life is not a sprint, it's a marathon. It's a race that is slow, steady and not simple. It's a race, however, that I'm able to run because of God's grace.

It has taken a lot of prayer and the support of the village that we always talk about, but the village was totally there for me. With God and my village, I have persevered...and because of God and my village, I believe that I am winning.

Chapter 1

I don't think there was a parent more proud than I as I sat in the Kennesaw College gymnasium and watched my son walk across the stage to receive his high school diploma. My son, my black son, my first born, Miles was on his way to do great things, I just knew it.

But then, just a few hours later after we'd had our celebration and were settling down at home, Miles told me the great things I wanted for him were going to be on hold for a little while.

"I won't be going to college," Miles said, shocking me. "I want to go to New York and find myself."

"Find yourself? You can find yourself in college." Miles had applied to several colleges and he'd been accepted at Alabama State.

But now, my son was telling me he had different plans.

"No, Mom. I can't. I want to go away and figure it all out."

I didn't want to just say, "Are you crazy?" So, I asked Miles to tell me more about his plans of finding himself.

My son had a good friend who was attending New York University at the time and he was doing very well.

"I'm going to stay with him, get a job, meet all the famous kids on social media and become famous myself," my son said.

Then, Miles smiled as if he really did have it figured out.

It didn't sound like a very solid plan to me, and while all I wanted to say to my son was, "Yeah, right," I knew I had to let him go. He was eighteen; he had to figure out life on his own.

Accepting that was one of the hardest things I ever had to do, but there was not much I could have done to stop him. My eighteen-year-old had his mind made up; he was excited and I was terrified. This was my son wanting to go out into the world on his own.

That's not what I wanted. What I wanted was to protect him and convince him that the best course of action was *not* to go to New York to become famous, but to go to college where he would get the kind of education that would help him make it in life. I wanted him to follow in my footsteps, at least when it came to his education.

But a couple of hours later, after the thought of Miles leaving Atlanta for New York had settled into my mind, I realized I was trying to force my dreams onto my son; I had to let him go so that he could find and live his own dreams.

Over the next few days, I watched him pack, not able to believe this was happening. But I didn't just sit and watch. He was still my son and I wanted the best for him. So I helped him. I went shopping and bought him several things that I thought he would need: underwear, socks, towels, and even though he'd be sleeping on a friend's couch, I bought him some bedding so he'd be comfortable.

Then, the time came. Just a couple of weeks after having earned his diploma, my son was ready to take off to New York. I clearly remember saying to Miles, "This is what I want you to know — if you're just going to New York to pursue some foolishness, I will not support you; you will be on your own. But if you're serious, then, I'll be here for you."

"Thanks, Momma," he said before we hugged.

Days later, he was on his way to Hartsfield-Jackson Atlanta International Airport. The good thing about this was that his father worked for an airline so Miles had flying privileges, which meant he could leave, but he could return home as well — thank God!

As I watched him walk toward the front door of our home that day, I wished I could take his hand and pull him back, but I knew I couldn't do that. He was an adult now, but he was also just like me — he was gonna do what he wanted to do anyway. So, I had to let this part of his life play out.

I think my son was in search of what he thought was his introduction into adulthood. I hoped he found what he was really looking for.

Watching him leave my house and truly letting him go was one of the hardest things I'd ever had to do.

*****

Kids never do what you tell them to do. Like they never call when they arrive at their destination the way they're supposed to. Waiting for Miles to call me that day was like waiting for paint to dry. After hours passed and I couldn't take it anymore, I had to make the first call. Even though I punched his number into my phone, I didn't want to have one of those mom attitudes when he answered; I didn't want to act bothered at all.

So, I called him. "Hey," I said. "What's going on? How's it going?"

"It's going good, Momma," he said.

"I'm glad you made it to New York safely."

"Yeah, I did."

We talked for just a little while longer; it had been a long travel day for him, so I told him I'd speak with him soon. Then, I hung up and I didn't feel any better. Letting him go was going to be so hard, but then, I knew God was looking out for me when I spoke to my best friend, Linda, the next day.

"I can't believe he's gone and staying up there in New York."

"I know, it's hard," she said, trying to console me, "but you know he's going to be all right. Miles is a good kid, he'll be fine."

"I know that," I said.

Linda asked, "Where's he staying?"

I gave her the address in Harlem where Miles would be with his friend and she said, "Oh my God, Venita. That's just one block from where Duncan and I live."

I sat up straight. "You're kidding." I couldn't believe it. One of my best friends in the world and her husband would be that close to Miles!

"This is perfect," Linda told me. "Now you really don't have to worry. Duncan and I will look out for him," she told me and I knew she was telling the truth.

Linda and I had been friends for over twenty years, since we'd met on the campus of Saint Augustine's College. So we'd had each other's backs for a long time and I knew she'd really have my back right now. Linda and Duncan didn't have children, but I knew they would treat mine as their own.

"Just let Miles know he can call on us for anything at any time," she said.

Linda had no idea how much relief and peace she'd just given to me. But that peace didn't last for very long.

Miles did stay with his friend, sleeping on his couch as he'd said he would. But the weeks, turned into a month, and then another and the whole time, I wasn't really sure what Miles was doing. He had applied for food stamps, so I didn't have to worry about him eating. But it seemed to me he wasn't doing much of anything beyond partying all night and playing video games. At least, that's what he seemed to be doing every time we talked. When I called him during the day, he was just getting up, or when I called at night, he was always heading out. It seemed to be a life of leisure rather than a life of purpose. This was definitely not the life that I had planned for him.

He *was* doing one of the things he said he would do — in New York, he was meeting those popular kids who seemed to own social media. You know the kids: the ones who were making moves in the music industry, the ones who were on popular reality shows, the ones whose families were always on television. He was making friends and cultivating relationships by any means necessary. That's what Miles was doing at night; he was hanging out with all of them.

Personally, I thought he was wasting God's good time. He didn't have a job yet, although he said he had interviews set up. That was what he needed — a job with good benefits where he could earn a decent living.

But although I wanted to get on that phone and not only tell Miles to come home, but tell him what to do with his life, I knew that couldn't happen. He was going to do his own thing and he had to find his own way.

So, I did what was best, I turned my son over to God, which seemed to be my daily ritual.

"Lord, you know what's best for Miles, so please take care of my son."

That's what I kept saying over and over. I had to keep saying it because I truly did want God to cover my son, but I also had to keep saying it because in my mind, I was the one who knew what was best for Miles. After all, I was his mother, right? I was the one who'd birthed him, right? And I had stretch marks to prove it.

But I stayed the course. I let my son do what he thought he had to do, and I kept praying he would see the light and come home.

The call I'd been waiting for came at the end of the summer. The phone rang and when I heard my son's voice, I smiled.

"Momma, I'm taking a flight back. I'm coming home."

"Okay," I said, hoping he didn't hear my excitement. My hope was that he was giving up that New York dream of finding himself and now, he would go to college. When I hung up the phone from him, I did my happy dance. Yes! There was a God! Won't He do it?

I was prepared to dip right into my 401k and get Miles off to college. It didn't matter how much it cost, I was going to do it. My in-laws were all in, too. They'd already told me they would help in any way they could and make sure Miles had everything he needed. With my village, I was going to do whatever it took!

My son, my firstborn, was going to college!

Chapter 2

We were approaching the end of the summer in 2015 and I was running all over Georgia getting my son ready to attend Alabama State University. He would be in Montgomery, Alabama, only a little more than two hours away from home, which to me was perfect.

Miles still wasn't as enthusiastic as I was about college. I think he felt like since things didn't pop for him in New York, he didn't really have too many options. Alabama State was his last resort. But I figured once he got to Alabama, he would love college, he would understand my dreams for him, and everything would be fine from there.

I wanted my son to have everything he needed

when he got to school, so he would have no complaints. I went on a spending binge. A Mac Book — check. A refrigerator — check. A microwave and a television — check and check. I had a long list and before we headed to Alabama, there was going to be a check by everything on it. Even though this was all last minute, I was unbothered by that. Nothing mattered except Miles going to college.

I knew I was behaving like a proud mom, and that was cool because that's what I was. My son was attending an HBCU, just like I'd done in the 80's. He was gonna get his college education and I already knew the advantages this would give him because I had experienced it all myself.

*****

I was from a small town in Indiana, Gary, and I'm sure no one would have ever heard of us if it hadn't been for the Jackson Five. But that famous singing group didn't change anything about Gary. We still had few options when we graduated from high school in 1986. Back then, I had three choices at graduation: I could work in the steel mill as most did, I could enroll in Uncle Sam's armed forces, or I could attend college. Out of those three options, I figured I'd give that college thing a try. I mean, it couldn't hurt, right?

Choosing college was one of the best decisions I'd ever made in my life. Attending college and earning my B.A. allowed me to compete in Corporate America. It was what was required then to have a good chance in this country, and it was required now if you truly wanted to be successful. I didn't think anyone could survive in today's times without a secondary education, so I was so happy for my son.

I had so many hopes for Miles. I wanted him to be able to compete in anything he wanted to do and attending college at Alabama State was the first step.

Looking back, I know all I was doing was trying to raise Miles the way I'd been raised. There's really nothing wrong with that, except that was very limited thinking. If we encourage our children to do just what we've done, that restricts them to life as we know it and there is so much more out there that's available to them today.

But back then, all I knew was college. That's all I knew for people who'd been successful. So with my limited experiences, that's what I wanted for my son.

It was early one morning in August when we packed that car and headed off to Montgomery. Can I tell you, I'd never been happier to get up and take a two hour drive? This was a celebration, of sorts...we took the entire family in two cars. In my car, I had Miles and my daughter, Nina, with me and his dad drove the other car with his parents. We were in pursuit of getting Miles checked into his dorm and settled into his college life.

I was so excited, but I may not have been the most excited. My in-laws were just as thrilled as I and completely on board the way they'd been his whole life. Again, they let me know they would there for any support (financial or spiritual) that was needed.

We arrived at the university around noon, found his dorm and then all of us unpacked the car, taking everything to Miles's room. When we first walked in, I paused. This was so different than the dorm I'd stayed in. At Saint Augustine's, I had the privilege of being in a new dorm.

But this — this was a room that felt empty, (except for the two beds and two desks) cold and old. I wasn't too concerned, though; we were about to change all of that. His roommate hadn't arrived yet, so

Miles chose his bed and then, we all got to work. We put his bedding on his bed, and began to help him unpack. We set up the refrigerator and it was when we hooked up his television that we decided to make a run to Walmart.

"I need a bigger TV," Miles said.

I felt the 32-inch was large enough, but if that was what Miles wanted, I was going to find the biggest TV I could. Listen, I was so happy my son was in college that I would have bought him three televisions if that's what he wanted.

Miles had some graduation money and I added to it to get him a 55-inch screen TV. Really, that should have been a clue for me. He was focused more on a television than walking around the campus; I should have known then that Miles had plans that were very different from mine.

When we returned with the bigger television, Miles's roommate was there with his mom and brother. We all introduced ourselves and I liked his roommate and his family right away. His roomie was a soft-spoken young man from South Georgia and I was pleased that he would be Miles's first friend in college. I hoped they'd become as close as brothers.

After another hour or so, it was time for us all to say our goodbyes and what was interesting was that I was having as hard a time leaving Miles in his dorm as I had watching him walk out of the door the day he'd gone to New York. That was surprising to me. I wanted him here in college — I guess letting go of my firstborn was never going to be easy.

As we drove away from the campus and headed up I-75 North, my heart was heavy and my hope was even heavier. I really wanted this for Miles and I hoped that after a few days, he'd want this as much as I did.

Inside, I said a silent prayer: *Lord, let Miles like Alabama State University and let these next four years be ones that will create wonderful, unforgettable memories for him.*

For a moment, I felt settled, but then, I added to my prayer: *And let him find a nice girl, Lord. A really nice girl who will become his wife, my daughter-in-law.*

After that, I felt even better. All was going to be well with my son.

Chapter 3

Miles had only been in school for about a week when the calls began coming in to me, one behind the other.

"Momma, I'm not supposed to be here."

"Momma, I'm supposed to be famous."

"Momma, I'm supposed to be rich."

"Momma, I'm supposed to be doing music."

Every time he complained to me, I'd hang up and pray, "*Lord, Jesus, help me!*" But to my son, my response was always the same: "You are supposed to be there, you have plenty of time to be famous, you have plenty of time to be rich. Right now, just go to class."

But my response didn't stop him. He continued to call, whine and complain:

"I'm supposed to be rich; I should be rich."

The phone calls kept coming, but no matter what I said, I couldn't settle my son down. Finally, I prayed to God, "*Lord, please just take the wheel. I can't do this any longer. I give this child back to you!*"

Not long after that prayer, a final call came from Miles. "Momma, they don't like me here and I don't like them. I'm leaving."

I shook my head. Miles hadn't given college a chance. He'd only been there for two months, but the way he sounded, I knew I wouldn't be able to change his mind. So all I said was, "Okay, Miles, if you do decide to leave, please just withdraw from school properly so you won't have any extra fees."

"Okay, Momma."

I felt like he was home before I hung up the phone because within a few days, my firstborn was back. He didn't even bring home most of his stuff; he just left it there when his dad drove down to get him.

My son left Alabama State and all that the university had to offer. He left what I thought would give him a secure future — he left all of that behind never to return.

Besides the fact that I was concerned about his

education, all I could think about was, "*Lord, here comes all the loud music and all of the guys in and out at my house.*"

I was absolutely right; that's what happened. Miles came home...back to my house, back to his room, back to his bed, and back to being in and out of my house and my car. Miles driving my 5 series BMW wasn't too big of a deal since, at the time, I was in pharmaceutical sales and had a company car. In the beginning, it was fine — at least for the first week or so.

But then as the weeks passed, it began to get to me. Especially the constant in and out of my house and the staying out very late at night. It was the staying out late that had me so nervous. I was a mom with a black son and when he was out in my car after dark, I worried; I still worry. That's why, like every other mom, I told Miles I didn't want him to be out at all hours of the night.

But no matter what I said, the nights with Miles got longer and later, and there were times when I just couldn't sleep. The challenge with that, though, was I couldn't afford not to get my rest. I couldn't afford to put all of my attention and energy into Miles. Not when I had another child; Nina needed my attention, too. And, I had a job that demanded a lot of my attention and senses, as well. As a sales person, I covered a lot of territory in Georgia, driving sometimes a hundred miles a day. To do this, I had to be of sound mind and body, and staying up late and worrying about my son's safety didn't give me any kind of peace at all.

I just couldn't imagine where Miles was going and staying out to all kinds of hours and so, after a few days, I asked him, "Where are you going every night? Why do you have to be out so late?"

"I'm in the studio. I'm doing my music."

"What music?" I asked.

"We're laying down tracks at the studio."

To this day, I cannot tell you where in the world (or where in Georgia) that studio was located. All I knew was that Miles went to the studio when he finally rolled out of bed sometime in the early afternoon, but then, he wouldn't return home until the wee hours of the morning, as my grandmother used to say.

Going through this with Miles was hard; I knew this process of my son finding himself was going to take some time and patience, but how could I watch him every day just going to the studio? What did that mean? He hadn't expressed a lot of interest in music before and now this was what he wanted to do?

See, when I was his age, I had only those three choices I mentioned earlier: working in the steel mill, going into the military, or attending college. But kids these days had way more opportunities. That was a good thing, really. I loved all the things that were available to young people now. This was a good time to be a young adult with what seemed to be endless opportunities.

If this was good for everyone else, I had to accept that it was good for Miles, too. My son had options. I had to realize the hope I had for him settling down in a secure nine-to-five was just not going to happen. I needed to get that thought out of my head and that hope out of my heart.

My kid was determined to explore all the opportunities in front of him that would ultimately get him to his dream — to be rich and famous.

Then one day, he told me a little bit more about this music. "I'm going to be a rapper, Momma."

I just shook my head, wondering where had this come from. If he'd come to me and said he wanted to be a photographer, I would get it. His dad was a successful celebrity photographer, so he'd be following in those footsteps. Or if he'd said he wanted to be a videographer, even that would have made sense to me. But a rapper?

"A rapper?" I finally said, letting him know that I was surprised.

"Yeah, Momma. I told you, I'm going to be famous. I'm gonna be a famous rapper."

"You told me you were going to be famous a long time ago. But you never said anything about being a rapper."

"Well, that's how I'm going to be famous."

Jesus, take the wheel! But all I said to him was, "Oh, okay."

Now mind you, Miles did attend a Performing Arts High School that had also been attended by Collin Sexton of the Cleveland Cavaliers, and a new up and coming rapper, Nas X. But Miles hadn't been part of anything that had to do with singing, acting and dancing.

Still, I just sat back because there was one thing I did know. Miles was young and if there was ever a time to pursue a dream, it was now while he had his whole life in front of him. So, I had to keep doing what I'd been doing; I had to continue to just support him, even though I didn't believe he was going to be successful at this.

There was no way I would tell him that, though. I would never take away his dream. He was the one who had to find out everything for himself.

The weeks passed, and nothing seemed to be happening to me. Miles kept the same schedule: waking up late, rolling out of bed and out of the house, then not returning until well after midnight.

All I could do was pray and pray and pray some more.

Chapter 4

And then, there were two!

My son had a habit of bringing new and sometimes interesting friends to our home. I never made a big deal out of it, that was just the way he was. Everyone was a friend of Miles.

That's why it was no surprise when he came home one evening with a guy and said, "Mom, meet my producer, Perry."

I said, "Producer? Producer of what?"

"You know, my music."

I nodded. "Oh, okay."

After all, he did come home a couple of weeks ago and introduce me to a kid he called his manager. I do remember his name started with a Z, so I guess it all made sense. I gave Perry a quick glance while I greeted him. The sand-colored complexion young man seemed to be about my son's age. He was very polite and so articulate, but after saying hello and chatting just a little bit, I left the two of them alone.

The next day, when I came home, Miles was there already. I knew he wanted to talk to me about something if he was home that early. "Momma, can Perry stay with us?"

This was going in the wrong direction. Miles had been home for about a month now, and he wanted to bring someone in to live with us? Really Miles?

I said, "Why do you want him to stay here?" I kept my voice low since Perry was back in Miles's bedroom. "Why doesn't Perry just go home?"

"He doesn't have a home, Momma," my son replied. "He's homeless. He's been staying in his car and I don't want him to do that; I want him to stay here, at our home."

Well, that made me feel bad. I didn't want to think of anyone living out of their car, especially not a young man like Perry. But I couldn't open our doors to everyone who didn't have a home. So, I asked Miles, "How do you know him?"

"We met at the studio a couple of weeks ago." Then, he went on to tell me the story about how Perry was recording at the studio, but the guys there weren't impressed with his sound. Miles had asked them more about Perry, but they'd tried to encourage him to just keep it moving and ignore Perry.

That was the wrong thing to say to my son. That made him step to Perry and ask if he could hear some of his beats. Miles liked what he heard and that led to their friendship. My son nor I knew, at that time, that Miles and Perry would one day become as close as brothers, and collaborate on their first hit song, "One Night."

After hearing Perry's story, there was no way I could put the kid out on the street. So I told Miles, "Okay, he can stay in your room with you."

"Thanks, Momma," Miles said.

"But don't get it twisted," I added. "He's going to help out around here just like you. He will help with whatever I need him to do."

"Yeah, Momma. Of course."

Just like that, I had two sons. Right away, though, it was clear to see that having Perry around wasn't bad at all. After all, I could get Perry to do chores quicker than I could get Miles. Anything I asked Perry to do: to take out the trash, to wash the dishes...whatever, it didn't matter. Perry was there to handle it.

However, even though I did enjoy having Perry there, he wasn't the answer to all the questions I had about what Miles was doing. The boys continued to keep those late hours, going to the studio night after night after night. All I kept thinking was how long was this going to last? Miles couldn't spend the rest of his life inside of a studio. He would have to do something else eventually. There had to be a job — with benefits — somewhere in his future.

Every time I talked to Miles about this, though, he kept assuring me I didn't have anything to worry about. "I have a plan, Momma."

The problem was I heard his words, but I didn't see any plan. All I saw was him at home (and in a stuudddiiiooo) doing nothing and nothing happening. What I really wanted to say to Miles was, "Okay, so when hanging out at the studio doesn't work, do you have a Plan B?"

I knew if I asked him that, though, my son would look at me like I was crazy and say, 'I don't need a

Plan B because A will work!'

Again, this was a difference between kids today and my generation. Kids today didn't think they needed a back-up plan when they were going to put everything into that first plan.

I have to say I do admire these kids for that and in a very real way, I admired my son. He was *so* sure of his dream. He was much happier now than when he'd been away at college. It was as if he absolutely knew he was doing the right thing. He knew this was his destiny.

He kept trying to reassure me. "Momma, I'm telling you; I'm about to be famous."

"Okay," I kept saying and I kept thinking the same thing, too. Like, 'Don't you know that everyone wants to be famous?' And, 'You only have a one in a million chance of that happening.'

Since I wasn't about to say that out loud, once again, all I could do was bow my head and pray to God. But this time, I had questions and I cried out to Him. *Lord, I gave this child back to you. What are you doing?*

I didn't get an answer and it was frustrating. But I should have known that God knew what He was doing. I was about to experience the beginning of what would absolutely change my life.

Chapter 5

My conversations with Miles were always the same.

"I have a plan, Momma. I'm going to be famous," he would say.

Then, I'd say, "Okay, Miles," and try not to let my frustration show. All I wanted him to see was my support.

But one day after I gave him my normal, "Okay, Miles," my son pulled out his cell phone. "Let me show you something, Momma." He scrolled through a few screens, then pulled up a website. "This is a streaming music site," he said, "and I uploaded one of my songs, "One Night," the one Perry produced for me. See these numbers?"

My eyes got wide as I took in the analytics. Not only did it show that hundreds of thousands of people had listened to Miles's music, but they liked what they'd heard.

I was in disbelief! This was amazing. Miles had only been home for about six weeks and before he'd shown me this video, that had seemed like a long time. But for him to have made these kind of inroads in that short amount of time, really was something. What was crazy about this was that while I supported my son, I'd never heard his music, but apparently hundreds of thousands of others had.

"And this is different music, Momma," Miles continued.

He was right. He really had his own sound. This sounded new and different and from the way the kids were downloading and listening to it, everyone seemed to like it.

"Okay," I said, this time feeling more assured.

When Miles walked out the room, I began to shift my thinking. Maybe I needed to take my son's Plan A a little more seriously. If he was really going to do this, if he was really going to sell his music, he could take off. There were things he'd need and the first thing was setting this up so he could legitimately do this as a business.

I filed all the papers to establish an LLC. (Although if I knew then what I know now...if I'd known Miles was going to make millions, I would have set up an S-Corp to get the better tax advantages.) But I set up his business and put everything in order so that financially, we'd be ready for whatever would happen.

Now, I had a little bit of a different attitude. When Miles and Perry hung out to all hours of the night, I knew they were really working. So we fell into a bit of a routine, where they kept their schedule and Nina and I kept ours.

Not too long after, Miles came to me with more news. "Guess what, Momma? I'm gonna be in Kanye's fashion show. The Season 3 Yeezy fashion show."

"Really? How did that happen?" I asked.

He explained that one of his friends, Ian Conner, was staffing Kanye West's fashion show that was coming up on Thursday in New York. Ian was a huge social media influencer. He and Miles had met in the airport, a few years before, had stayed in touch and were now good friends. He wanted Miles to be in Kanye's show.

"That sounds interesting," I said after Miles explained it to me. "How much are they paying you?"

"They're not, but I really want to go. It'll be a great opportunity for me to get exposure."

"Okay," I said. Ever since he'd shown me his song on that website, I'd been more serious about this for my son. I wasn't concerned that Miles had to go to New York. His flying benefits were definitely paying off now, allowing him to be a frequent flyer at no cost.

A few days later, Miles was on stage at Madison Square Garden for Kanye West's Yeezy Fashion Show.

I was the proudest mom ever, sitting front and center. I wasn't front and center in the Garden; the show was being streamed on Tidal (mind you, I had no idea what Tidal was!) and I was watching it live, sitting right in my car.

The models included Naomi Campbell and Kylie Jenner, but Ian and Miles were standing right up front with Miles wearing a fire engine red Yeezy sweater matching his hair to his Yeezy sweater. And Ian was beside him wearing blond locs that matched his goldish Yeezy sweater.

That made me smile — my son with his red hair that he had all because of me. It had started when he was sixteen years old, the summer between his junior and senior year in high school. Miles got an interview for a summer job at McDonald's and I was more excited than he was....

"Oh, my goodness, Miles, this is your first job."

"Yeah," he said with much less enthusiasm than I had.

Coming from the corporate world, I wanted to make sure my son had the best advantage. So I wanted him to go in there dressed to impressed with black slacks, a crisp white shirt — and then, his hair...that was going to be a little bit of a challenge.

My son had been wearing braids, but I knew those braids weren't going to work; they weren't the right corporate look. Even though Miles would be working at McDonald's, it was still one of the largest corporations in the country.

"You're going to have to cut your hair," I told Miles.

My son looked at me like I'd grown two heads. "I don't wanna cut my hair. My hair is what makes me different."

"You have to," I said. "This is a company and you want to make the best impression with your first impression. We're

going to have to shape your hair up a bit."

It took a little more time, but I was finally able to convince him, and Miles cut his braids. He got the job and I was so excited. But Miles was not. After working there only two weeks, Miles told me:

"Momma, this job sucks. I cannot believe people work here to pay their bills with this little bit of money."

It wasn't long after that when Miles quit. He was just in high school, so I gave him a pass. But then, when fall rolled around and Miles was about to begin his senior year, he was not happy with me.

"You made me cut my hair," he said as if that was now the worst thing ever and it was all my fault. "Now, I'm going to look like everyone else. Man, Momma, now I won't look different."

Miles went on and on and on. He complained and complained and complained. It got to be so much that I finally threw up my hands and said, "You wanna look different, go dye your hair red or something." I shook my head hoping that would shut him up.

It shut him up all right — the next morning, my son's hair was red! A fire red! I mean, Bozo the Clown red! I couldn't believe it. I hadn't meant for him to really dye his hair. I was just trying to get him out of my face and to stop complaining.

Well, he was different all right. And as his hair grew out, he let his braids get longer and then, he started adding the beads. All I could do was shake my head. My son was happy, thinking that he was being original. Little did he know that we'd seen this look before on an artist of our times. An artist known as Rick James.

Once he dyed his hair, Miles went all the way, changing his persona, too. He now wanted to be known by his nickname, Lil Yachty that he'd been given a few years before. When he was in high school, there were a group of older kids who called themselves, "The Yacht Club," and Miles wanted to be part of that group. Those guys dressed well, and finally, they asked Miles to join them. But they told him that because he was the youngest, he'd be Lil Yachty. Later, came his alter ego, Lil Boat.

Now, as I watched him on the stage in the Yeezy fashion show, wearing that shirt that matched his red hair, it seemed that his hair color and his name had paid off. I loved the way Miles stood out. It may not have been my intention to have him walking around with red hair, but it was part of who my son was now.

I thought the fashion show was wonderful, but what was even better was the press the next morning. Oh my, the press was amazing, just amazing. When all the morning shows, including *Good Morning America,* reviewed the show from the night before, Miles was front and center in all the playback videos. His face was everywhere, including the Adidas website.

If I thought I'd been proud the night before, it was even better in the morning. It felt like Miles was really beginning to be on his way. The dreams that he had for himself were coming true.

Chapter 6

Kanye's Yeezy Season 3 was a hit!

The following morning Miles's face was all over the place and he was getting good exposure. His name recognition wasn't just coming from the fashion show. His song, "One Night," the one that had been produced by Perry continued to do very well. So between the fashion show and his song, it really did begin to feel like it was all beginning to come together.

I was cautiously excited, starting to see for myself the same dream that Miles had, but I wasn't getting too far ahead of anything. I knew we needed to take this slowly, really focus on this one day at a time. I kept the Lord front and center, continually asking for His direction and praying that not only would God cover Miles and provide him with the right opportunities, but that He would make sure the right people came across our path.

In the city, the buzz about Miles continued to grow. His song was being streamed more and more and soon, he came to the attention of other artists who wanted to meet with him to possibly do business or as the kids would say, "sign him."

We were hearing the same thing from people around town about Miles: "This kid has potential." There was so much attention given to my son that now, I was becoming a true believer. I knew Miles was about to level up.

"Don't sign anything," I continuously warned him. "Don't put your signature on a single thing."

"I won't, Momma," he assured me.

My only hope was that Miles would listen to me. I didn't know where this was going with my son, but I wanted the very best for him and I wasn't sure if he knew what it could mean if he signed off on a bad contract. There were so many horror stories out there and I didn't want my son to be the star in any kind of messed up story.

With the way people were meeting with Miles,

telling him he had potential and that he could be their next big deal, that meant signing on the dotted line. Because of all the buzz, I went into full gear. I had been telling Miles not to sign anything because I didn't want him in a bad contract, but what was a bad contract? It wasn't like I really knew. We were getting into the field of money and legalities and if I wanted the best for my son, the first thing I had to do was find him the best legal counsel around.

I started by asking my friends, "Do you know of a good entertainment attorney?" Then, from their referrals, I began making calls.

The first attorney wanted a large retainer up front. That didn't sit well with me since I wasn't sure of what we would be getting in exchange for that fee. I made a few more calls and even contacted a well-known Atlanta attorney who had represented several Atlanta artists.

"I would love to work with you, Ms. McCollum, but unfortunately, my schedule is full right now."

It seemed like this was going to be tougher than I expected and finally, I reached out to Shannon, Miles's dad who was a celebrity photographer. We weren't the best of friends, but we'd managed to co-parent without too much confusion.

Shannon was the perfect person to reach out to because he had lots of ties to the city of Atlanta. First of all, this was where he'd been born and raised so he seemed to know everybody; he had made thousands of connections over the years through his work.

He had taken photos of some of Atlanta's hottest artists such as Xscape, Goody Mobb, Ludacris, Andre 3000, Big Boi, Lil Jon, just to name a few of the local celebrities; but his reach was far beyond the city. He'd photographed Erykah Badu, Jill Scott and even two presidents: President Jimmy Carter and then, President Barack Obama himself.

Currently, he was on tour with George Lopez and his comedy tour that included Cedric the Entertainer, D.L. Hughley, and several other comedians.

It made perfect sense for me to reach out to him. I figured he'd know someone who could help.

"Actually, I do know of someone," Miles's dad told me after I explained the situation. "Let me reach out to Attorney Vince."

He was a local attorney, but he never returned Shannon's call. So, Shannon reached out to a high school classmate, Uwonda Carter. After their graduation, she'd attended Georgia State, while he was at Clark Atlanta University. They ran in the same social circles and he knew she'd attended law school. Not only that, he knew she was into the hip hop culture from all the friends they had in common.

"All we can do is try," Shannon said to me. "I'll give her a call and get back to you."

He left a message for Uwonda and she returned his call right away. He set up a meeting for us to meet at Shannon's parents' home in East Point a few days later.

I walked into that meeting prepared, with a list of questions I was going to ask. I was ready to interview her, just like she was going to interview us. From my research, I'd found out that Uwonda represented quite a few artists. But I wanted to see not only her knowledge of the industry for myself, I wanted to see if she knew about Miles. I wanted to know if she had done her homework and if she had, did she have a vision of where my son would fit in.

Walking into that meeting, I was prepared; walking out of that meeting, I was satisfied. First of all, Uwonda really knew her stuff. Like I said, she'd represented other top artists, so not only did she really know this industry, but she had contacts, too. She would represent my son well.

But it was more than just the professional side. Something I always looked for was a person's energy and Uwonda had it. She was as excited as I was about Miles and I knew she would look out for him no matter what. When she agreed to work with us, I was pleased.

It turned out that every instinct I had about Uwonda at that meeting was right. We've developed a wonderful working relationship and not only has it been a joy to work with her, but I trust her as a member of our team. The importance of this is something that I discuss later in the book because I didn't know this then, but I certainly know this now — having the right energy and chemistry is almost as important as a person's knowledge. You are going to be working with people who will have your child's future in their hands and at times, you will be at their mercy. You have to choose wisely and you have to choose the best.

Uwonda did require a small retainer to get started, but what she required made sense to me. We were able to cover that fee, and then, we all got to work!

*****

It seemed as if every day Miles came home with new buzz — someone else wanted to sign him. The first artist who was interested in signing him offered Miles $44,000. When Miles told me that, all I could do was frown. We were in this for the long haul and that didn't sound like a lot of money — not that I knew a lot about the industry, but I knew something about business and that offer seemed pretty low.

The offers kept coming, though they were never accompanied by any paperwork, just talk. And I was waiting for the right person to make the right offer. But while I was waiting, Miles had his eyes set on a local managing team in Atlanta.

"Momma, I know where I want to be and I keep seeing him around the city at all of these parties."

"Who?" I asked Miles. "Who are you talking about?"

"Coach K."

I guess the other manager was out, I thought.

Miles continued, "I keep seeing him, but I never get a chance to talk to him." Miles's went on to tell me how he'd tried to make eye contact whenever they saw each other, but the opportunity for the two to connect directly never presented itself.

"I tried to DM him, but I never heard back," Miles said.

Once Miles mentioned the name Coach K, he didn't need to say anymore. Everyone knew Kevin Lee or Coach K, as he was fondly known in the hip-hop community.

I didn't know Coach K personally, but there were a few ways in which we were kind of connected. Coach K and I had both attended Saint Augustine's College, though I was a few years older than he was. So when he was coming in, I was headed out. And we were both from Indiana; he was from Indianapolis. But those two things weren't enough for me to just try to walk up to him.

If I could get a formal introduction, I had a feeling that would be the start of something big for Miles. Coach K had managed two of Atlanta's biggest hip hop stars: Young Jeezy and Gucci Mane.

Besides being with his talent management firm, Solid Foundation, he was the Chief Operating Officer of Quality Control, also known as QC - one of the hottest labels in the country. He was guiding the careers of a few young hip hop stars.

I contacted a good friend of mine to introduce me to Coach K directly, though I still wasn't sure if an introduction this way was going to work. All day, every day, kids were seeking out Coach K, and I imagined dozens of people walking up to him, trying to talk him into giving them that big break. How would an introduction by my friend be any different from what Coach had to deal with all the time?

While I was trying to figure it out, Miles was having the same conversation with his father that he'd had with me. He told his dad he wanted to be part of Solid Foundation and Quality Control. Miles and I were both shocked when his father told us he knew Coach K.

"I've been working with him for a long time," he said.

I was surprised, but I shouldn't have been. He had Coach K's number locked into this phone and after a couple of calls, a few days later, Miles, his dad, Coach K and I were all on a conference call.

While Coach K was surprised to find out that Miles was the son of Shannon McCollum, the photographer he'd been working with for years, I was surprised to find out that Coach K was very much aware of Miles.

"Oh, I know exactly who your son is," he told me and Miles's father.

In that moment, I had a feeling that this phone call was about to change all of our lives.

Chapter 7

Days later, we were sitting in the Atlanta offices of Quality Control's home office, but it didn't feel like it was getting off to a good start to me. Shannon and I sat there with Coach K, and we all waited for Miles!

When my son showed up an hour late, I wanted to shake him and say, 'Boy, haven't I taught you anything!'

But Coach K didn't seem bothered at all by that, so I said nothing.

Once again, Coach K expressed how surprised he was that Miles was Shannon's son. "I had been contemplating reaching out to Miles," he said. "I still have the messages he sent to me on social media and thought we should talk." He shook his head again.

"Small world."

After that, we got down to business. We sat and talked for what would turn out to be hours, about all the possibilities for Miles's future.

"I'm very intrigued by this new sound that Miles has," Coach K told us. "That's what I do. I'm open to whatever music mania the young people are listening to."

Of course, that pleased all of us.

"And this is really a great time to be with QC," Coach K said. "We have the means to take your career to new heights," he said to Miles. He explained that at that moment, they had Migos, Young Greatness, and also Skipper Da Flipper at their label, so this was a perfect time for Miles to come on board.

Coach K already had a great reputation, but I personally got good vibes from the meeting — he had that good energy I was talking about earlier. But Coach K wasn't in this business alone. He was the COO and there was a CEO who was the other side of this dynamic duo — Pierre Thomas.

I wanted to meet with "Pee," as everyone called him, myself. Yes, everyone was talking about QC, but I was that protective Mama Bear. I needed to understand and see if there was *real* interest in my son. Would everyone on this team really get behind him? I didn't want him signed and then, nothing happened. That would be worse than not being signed at all.

It wasn't that I didn't trust Coach K or doubted Quality Control's capabilities. It was just that like I said before, there were so many horror stories, including a few stories with this label.

Like every other meeting I'd ever had, I walked into this meeting prepared, having done my research. I'd heard a few things on the streets about Coach K. He'd had his success with artists who'd made lots of money. But the artists had gotten caught up in stuff that wasn't all fun and games. As he sat there with us, though, Coach K was very honest in what had gone down with past relationships with artists.

"You're right," he said when I brought it up. "It isn't always pleasant and I've had to part ways with artists. I don't mind doing that if I have to. I do what's best for the artist and for the label."

Although everything Coach K told me was public information, I appreciated hearing it from the source and was grateful that he was so truthful. I wanted to give him a fair chance and get to know him for myself.

I wanted to give him the chance to show and prove what he could do.

After about an hour, Miles decided that his work was done and he was ready to exit. He knew Mom had it under control as usual. Once Miles left, Shannon and I got down to the real business with Coach and asked all the tough questions. I knew these kinds of chances didn't come along often and I had to get it right.

I had a list:

"What do you really want with my child?"

"What can you do for him?"

"Do you have a vision for him?"

"Where do you see this going?"

"What's the current state of QC?"

"What's the current status of Solid Foundation?"

"What time frame are we looking at?"

"How safe is the studio?"

"Will the studio be available for Miles at any time?"

"Will he have to pay for the studio?"

"What else do you guys have going on?"

What was great was that Coach K sat there and answered every one of my questions with patience and clarity. He wasn't pressed at all and it felt like he was glad I was going to be involved with Miles like this.

I walked out of that meeting feeling more than a little good; I felt like this was right.

*****

Coach K's reputation proceeded him, but when I left QC's headquarters, I knew for myself that this guy knew what he was doing. What was best was that Coach K was a leader. In his mid-40s, he'd been through some things and that, along with his honesty and his frankness made him a good example for the young men he worked with; I thought he'd be a great mentor for Miles. In his gray beard, you saw all the wisdom he had, but he also had that hip-hop swag that the young people admired and Miles loved and adored.

Even though I really liked Coach K, I couldn't say that I was 100 percent sold yet; I couldn't be — not until I had the chance to meet Pierre, the other half of QC. I had to make sure everyone was on board with Miles.

In the meantime, though, everything seemed to be working in my son's favor. First, Miles was really feeling what was going on right now. I hadn't seen my son so upbeat and positive, especially during our meeting with Coach K. It was easy to see that Quality Control was definitely where Miles wanted to be. Things were lining up even with our attorney. Uwonda was communicating with QC for two other artists she represented, so the professional relationship was already established.

A few weeks later, Miles was selected to perform for a campaign which encouraged young people to say NO to tobacco. The tobacco company had reached out to Miles through QC. They knew Miles didn't smoke and thought he'd be a great role model to spread awareness of their message.

The campaign was designed to stop kids from smoking. It included a commercial, print ads and Miles even did some mini concerts, where he was the headliner, that were free to the public.

This would be the beginning of a long list of campaigns and endorsements that would come my son's way. But what stands out most for me about this — this was the day that I finally met Pierre "Pee" Thomas.

We had stopped by QC to pick up tickets for the

concert for the campaign that was being held downtown. There was a group of us who'd gone to the offices: me and my daughter and a few friends along with Shannon, who we met there. We were all standing outside talking to Coach K when Pee pulled up. The moment he got out of his car, Coach introduced us.

Pee and I looked each other in the eye, and we shook hands. It was very formal, but this was all business to me.

Pee told me, "When I first heard the tape of Miles, I wasn't quite sure where he would fall in our line-up. But I knew that he was about to create his own lane and we're really excited about it."

I had a good vibe with Pee, just like I had with Coach K. One of the reasons was the way they interacted. The two men had a kind of big brother/little brother relationship that I admired and appreciated. Coach K was the older of the two, but they had a relationship where I could tell the respect went both ways. I really liked that, believing that each was bringing their own strengths to the team.

While we were meeting, they took me on a tour of the headquarters. I was impressed with the facility and

I could tell from all the equipment, that these men had invested their money into this business and that was great for thcir artists. The studio was large, with several rooms where the artists could record. But what I loved best were the security cameras that were throughout. At least when Miles was out at late night recording sessions, my child would be safe. I could tell that Coach K and Pee were not about the shenanigans; just anybody was not going to be walking up into QC. That was not going to happen.

When I walked out of this second meeting I felt more reassured than ever. These two men were building quite an empire; and they had a story to tell. What was so great was they assured me my son would be a part of their empire and their story and they would definitely take his career higher.

The decision was made. Now, it was time to get into the business of building my son's career.

Chapter 8

It was time to seal the deal. If Coach K was going to be Miles's manager, we needed to make it official and get an offer in writing.

"I really like working with Coach K," Miles told me. "That's who I want."

I loved the fact that my son had someone like Coach K to sign with; I loved their connection. So I agreed and Uwonda began negotiations with them. She reviewed all the paperwork because just like every job offer I'd ever accepted, I wanted everything in writing to protect all the parties involved. By March, 2016, a management deal was made and my son was signed to Solid Foundation.

What did this mean? It meant that Coach K was

now Miles's official manager. It meant that we now had a pilot flying this plane, navigating Miles's career in hopes that we would get a real deal.

While we were pleased and in the end everything worked out beautifully for us, having Coach K as both Miles's manager and his record label — I'm not sure that was the best choice. I really didn't understand what this meant for Miles and looking back, I'm not sure this was the smartest move on the chessboard. Again, this worked out for us, but it's not something I would recommend and I will discuss that later in the book.

Quality Control was in a partnership with Capitol Records, so once Coach K signed Miles to Solid Foundation, QC had to present Miles to Capitol for a record deal. Even though this really seemed to be happening, I still didn't know what to expect. All I could do was trust the process.

As the days went by, Miles spent even more time in the studio. Since he was now with Solid Foundation, he and his crew had free rein, being able to come and go to the studio as they pleased. He was at the QC studios daily, laying down tracks, working with Perry and other friends he'd rallied up to be on his team. Miles called them his sailing team since his alter ego was Lil Boat. The sailing team was appropriate so that he could name all his artists signed to his label — once he got his own label. That was always the goal; for an artist to get their own label. Miles was already preparing to feature his friends on his first album and include them on his first tour.

Miles's following continued to grow, especially with Coach K now at the helm. But Miles was doing a lot of it on his own, too. He had a strong social media presence and Coach K said it was all good — all of this he could take to Capitol and use as leverage to get Miles the best deal.

In the meantime, though, Coach K didn't want Miles just sitting around waiting as the deal with Quality Control/Capitol Records was being put together. Coach K and Pee decided it was a good idea to get Miles on the road for extra exposure. They paired Miles up as the opening act for a great up and coming rapper, Young Thug, and just 30 days after signing on with Solid Foundation, Miles was off on his first tour.

This was wonderful for Miles. Young Thug already had an amazing fan base and this would give his fans a chance to hear Miles and become fans of my son. The tour was mostly in small venues, in 15 cities, and they traveled from venue to venue and city to city by vans.

It was exciting but a bit nerve-wracking for me to think of my son out there on the road for the first time. Neither Miles nor I knew what to expect and of course, you know me by now — I had all of these horror stories in my mind. But Coach K went out with him to every stop, giving guidance and making sure a young man like Miles didn't get too far out there.

Once again, I was so grateful for this partnership. Coach K and Pee were doing everything they'd promised me when it came to Miles. They were giving him exposure to take his career higher, but they were giving him protection, too. They gave me peace beyond measure. I could sleep at night!

I wasn't involved too much in that first tour. This was new to all of us and I didn't want to overstep my boundaries. So, I stayed out of the way, but at the same time, I did stay involved. After all, this was Miles's future so I watched everything while the management company handled it.

The tour was sold out every night; the fans showed

so much love and I was so proud. My daughter and I were able to travel to Chicago for the last stop of Miles's tour. Before we went to the arena, we stopped by to see my dad. I had really hoped he would be able to go to the concert with us, but he wasn't up to it health wise.

So, Nina and I went and we met Miles's dad and some of our cousins there. It was amazing to see my son on the stage and the fans reacting to him with so much love. I couldn't have been more pleased for, or more proud of my son. Watching him on the stage was just confirmation that this kid was made for this. There were so many times when I shook my head in awe? Who knew? There was an answer to my question — God knew!

At the end of the show, I convinced Miles to go see his grandfather, and he did. He took time out of his busy schedule to make sure he saw his grandpa and I'm so glad that he did. Shortly thereafter, my dad's health began to decline even more; Miles had a chance to see him while he was well.

It was an exciting time. Miles had just released his second mixed tape, "Summer Songs 2," so we were all hyped about that. But nothing was more exciting than what happened on June 10th, just three months after Miles's tour began. The deal was ready to close and we had to go to Los Angeles to meet with all the powers that be. We had the full team: Miles, his dad, Coach K, Pee, Uwonda and I all flew out to L.A. We were all nervous, but excited at the same time and ready to do this.

Uwonda had been in this with us all the way, so we knew a little about what to expect in terms of money. All we had to do was sign on the dotted line.

That's what Miles did. He signed a joint record deal with Quality Control and Capitol Records the next day in the famous and historic round Capitol Records office building in Hollywood, California.

Even though this had been what we were working toward, now that it was finally here, it was a little hard to believe. It was surreal, and really, it hadn't taken very long; it wasn't even a year. But Miles had a dream, he went for it and now, my son was a rapper, signed to a major label with a major deal.

Little did I know, I had really raised a rapper!

Chapter 9

Miles had signed this big deal, but he was still living in my house. Now that he had a deal, though, he was more than ready to leave.

"I'm going to look for my own place," he said over and over.

The thing was, while my son was eighteen and he'd been living in New York and on tour, I still wasn't ready for this. I couldn't imagine my son out there, in his own place, on his own. He had never paid a bill, probably didn't know all the bills that went into a household; he just had no idea what life would be like living on his own.

Somehow, I did get Miles to listen to me about not being ready for his own place, at least for now. But the car, that was a different story. We had already decided that once he received his signing money, he would buy his first car. He really wanted a Mercedes G-wagon, so that was what it was! He and I went shopping together and that was his first big purchase.

He was so happy, and frankly, so was I. He really hadn't been driving all that long and now he had his own car, and a very nice one at that.

Once again, I was a proud mom.

But once he had that car, I had a feeling that Miles wasn't going to let the discussion about moving out on his own rest. And he didn't.

"Momma, I'm going to look for my own place," he began saying again a few months later.

He said it so much that I finally had to admit what I didn't want to. I had to give in to the realization that my son wasn't a little boy anymore. He was a young man who had found his way. He was at the beginning of living his dream, becoming more and more of a celebrity every day. His following was growing by leaps and bounds and with all of that going on with him, there was no way I could keep him at home forever.

Finally, I gave in and got on board with this idea of

Miles moving out. "Okay," I said, "and I'll help you find a nice place."

I got in touch with Coach K and he introduced me to his cousin, who was a real estate agent. He talked to Miles and then, the two of them hit the streets. He took Miles to about four, maybe five units, but Miles fell in love with a penthouse in Midtown.

So after a couple of weeks and a couple of signatures, my son had his own place. His first place — a two bedroom, three bathroom two level penthouse unit in one of the most popular areas in Atlanta. His neighbors were another popular rapper and an Atlanta Falcons player.

It was a good time for Miles, but it was moving so fast to me. My baby was leaving my house and I had a feeling that he would never look back. The only thing I could take solace in was that my son wouldn't be alone. Perry would be moving in with him, taking the extra bedroom.

However, as we prepared for the move, I found myself in that sad space again. It was hard to let him go, even if I was still doing so much for him.

I got him moved in and settled in after I bought all of his furniture, everything from the living room set to the patio set. From their linen to the forks and spoons. I made sure all of his photos from his tour were on the wall, wanting their place to feel like a home right away. (So much for independence, huh?)

It took me two weeks to do all of that and finally, I could turn my attention back to my home where I was about to make his bedroom my new closet. I had a walk-in closet in my bedroom, but it had been busting at the seams for a while. I didn't waste any time doing that and for a moment, it did make me feel better about Miles being gone.

I just had to accept it. My children were both growing up.

*****

I was still working while all of this was happening for Miles. My employer knew a little about what was going on in terms of my son being a rapper, but I don't think anyone at my company realized all the possibilities, especially since I continued with everything at work as if it was just business as usual.

But then, Miles began to get even more exposure with his song playing constantly on the radio. It was then that his success really came to the attention of my employer. Once everyone at the company realized the extent of what was going on with Miles, I began to get the feeling that my boss (and everyone else there) thought I would soon be leaving the company and when I did, I'd leave them high and dry.

That was never my intent; I planned to do my job to the end. Now of course, I did hope that one day, I would be able to work with my son, but Coach K had given me some good advice.

"Hold on, Vee," he said right after Miles signed his contract. "You'll be able to leave one day, just hold on."

Now, don't get me wrong; I enjoyed working, I enjoyed my job. I loved earning my own money, especially since I had bills, real bills: a mortgage, a car payment, utilities and two children I had to feed and clothe. Working had never been what I chose to do since I was fifteen years old.

But there was a reason why I was looking forward to the day when I'd be able to work with my son. It began seven years ago when one morning, I awakened with a tingle in my arm. I ignored that feeling because after I woke up, the tingle slowly subsided. But then, the next morning I woke up with the same feeling, though this time it was a bit painful. Again, I ignored it, just like I did every morning for the next three weeks.

Finally, I had to do something because the symptoms weren't going away. All of the doctors I talked to as I worked, told me I needed to see someone. As I explained my symptoms, I asked all of them, "What do you think it could be?"

No one could give me a diagnosis without an exam. Most said, "It doesn't sound like a heart attack or stroke, but you should go in and have it checked out as soon as you can."

I didn't listen to that advice; I didn't go in right away. For some reason, I thought I could ignore it and the symptoms would go away. I couldn't ignore it anymore, however, when one morning I awakened not only with the painful tingling, but with my fingertips being numb, too.

Now I knew for sure something was not right and I had to get to the doctor as soon as possible. I called my primary care physician, told her everything that was going on and she gave me her next available appointment, which was the following week.

When I got into her office, she talked to me a bit, then did a regular exam, taking all of my vitals. "What do you think it is?" I asked her when she finished all of that.

She shook her head. "I don't know. What I'm going to do is send you for a spinal MRI. That will tell us exactly what's going on."

With a sigh, I nodded. Even though I'd waited all of this time, now I wanted to know what was happening to me. But I understood I had to go through the process and the MRI was scheduled for two days later.

That morning, when I walked into the facility for the test, I had to admit I was a bit anxious. I'd had x-rays, of course, but I'd never had an MRI and this was scary. I had to lay inside of the large, tube-like machine that would create a detailed image of my spine. It felt cramped and made me feel claustrophobic.

It didn't take very long, maybe about thirty minutes. At the end of the MRI, I was told I'd have the results in a week. A week? I didn't want to wait that long, but I had to. A week later when my doctor called me, I braced myself, but I was so ready to find out what was wrong.

However, all she was able to say to me was, "Well, Ms. McCollum, there's not much I can tell you."

Her words confused me. Had something gone wrong with my test? "What do you mean?" I asked her.

"I don't have a diagnosis for you from the MRI."

"What? What's wrong? What happened?"

"I'm sorry, but I can't tell you much from your results. We do see a spot on your spine, but that could be anything. I'm going to send you to a neurologist."

Another doctor? "Okay," I said and then took down all the information for the referral.

A few days later, I was back in a doctor's office, this time with the neurologist. This doctor did all the talking, asking me so many questions. After spending about an hour with him, he said, "I'm going to send you for a brain and spinal MRI."

"Another MRI? You don't have any idea what it could be?"

He shook his head. "That's why I want you to have the test, this time we'll do it at the hospital. I can tell you that it's probably one of three things: a tumor, a vitamin or nutrient deficiency, or it could possibly be

MS, but I don't think it's that because you're forty-six. Believe it or not that's a little too old for multiple sclerosis. MS is something that's usually detected at a much earlier age. But instead of sitting here and wondering, I want to send you for testing and we'll go from there."

This was getting to be too much. I was already under a lot of stress at work; being in sales always came with so much stress because of the pressure to perform. There were always sales targets and the natural competition in the office. The competition was consistent and persistent and I worked hard to stay in the front of the line.

So I already had the stress of work, and now the stress of knowing that something was wrong with me, but having no idea whatsoever what that something was. After going over it in my mind, I did what I always did — I turned it over to God.

I had the two MRIs and then, the next week, I was scheduled to meet with the neurologist in his office. As I sat in the waiting room, flipping through magazines, I had to take a couple of deep breaths to calm myself from the anxiety that was rising inside of me. It had been weeks now, most of it was my fault for waiting so long. Still, I wanted to know now.

"Ms. McCollum, the doctor will see you now," one of the receptionists told me.

I took a deep breath as I followed her back to a patient room to wait for the doctor to bring the results. It seemed like I waited for hours, but it really was a short time before he came in. All I wanted to do was get this over with.

The doctor said, "I have good news and I have bad news. The good news is that you're going to live."

I exhaled a long breath.

"But the bad news is...you do have Multiple Sclerosis."

What? I leaned back a bit in the chair; I was shocked. Multiple Sclerosis, or MS, is a long lasting disease that can affect the brain, the spinal cord and the optic nerves. It can cause problems with vision, balance, muscle control and other basic body functions. The effects of the disease are different for everyone who's been diagnosed with MS.

The doctor continued, "You actually have been living with MS for quite some time. I was able to see some old lesions on your brain and of course, I see some existing ones. I can also see where the future lesions will be. So, I want you in a hospital bed tomorrow."

His words came at me quickly, making my mind swirl with all kinds of thoughts. I had multiple sclerosis? That just didn't seem possible. And now, he wanted me to check myself into a hospital by tomorrow? That was impossible.

"Doctor, I can't do that tomorrow. I have so much to do to get ready. I have to inform my employer, I have two children, I have so much to take care of before I can go into a hospital."

"Okay, I understand that," he said. "So then, I want you in the bed the day after tomorrow. We want to start treating you for this immediately."

That wasn't too much time, but I heard the urgency in his voice. "Okay," I said, agreeing to that.

I walked out of there feeling like my head was going to explode with two major thoughts — I had MS *and* I had to get to the hospital. Once I recovered from those thoughts, I went into action.

The first thing — I would need help. So, I called one of my closest friends, Regena Willis. Regena and I had been friends since middle school and now, she lived in Indianapolis. When I told her my situation, she agreed to come right away. That was a big relief because I had no doubt that Regena would take the best of care of me. With her there, she'd take everything off my plate: she'd take the kids to school, she'd do the grocery shopping, she'd keep my life organized.

Now, I was able to focus on my health. After Regena got settled in my place, she took me to the hospital two days later where once I was admitted, the doctor talked to me about the protocol — how they were going to treat my illness.

"This may sound a little strange," one of the doctors said to me, "but it's like we have to break your body down to build it back up." Then, he explained how they were going to pump me with steroids, needing to get those into my system to fight the MS. Next, they were going to change my diet, getting me on a gluten-free regiment.

The road was not easy; my body reacted to the steroids, of course, and I felt and looked like I had a stroke. My arm wouldn't straighten out and for days, it didn't feel like I was getting better. But, I remembered what the doctor had said — they had to break my body down to build it back up.

It was a scary time; I didn't know what to expect moving forward. Only God knew and I trusted God. That was all I could do.

I was released from the hospital five days later, but I was nowhere near being well. Regena was still there, promising she would stay with me for the long haul and I was so grateful because I didn't know how long it would take me to get back on my feet. I didn't have the energy to do much, and between low energy and my physical therapy, I had no idea when I'd begin to feel well enough to take back over my life.

However, the time didn't matter to Regena. My sisterfriend was right there. Regena took care of everything in my home, while she nursed me back to health.

It was long, it was hard, but I made it through. I had a full recovery and today, I'm operating at full capacity. Because of God's grace, I'm here today to tell my story.

What I learned during that time was that much of what I was dealing with had been caused by stress. There were things I had to do, including changing my diet and getting on an exercise regiment. Oh, and I had to watch my stress levels.

So fast forward to Miles and his success. Needless to say, what was happening to him came at such a perfect time. About a year after Miles signed his contract, I was able to leave corporate America. And today, I work for my son. I'm the manager who manages the other managers.

I'm also the Mom Manager who tells her son, "No more jewelry! No more cars!" I'm the Mom Manager who asks her son, "Who's that girl? We've got to pay our taxes." And I'm the Mom Manager who shakes her head and commands, "Don't buy another dog, please!"

Can I tell you how much of a blessing working with Miles has been for me?

I am very much aware that at the beginning of this journey, I didn't believe. At the beginning, I wanted Miles to live out my plans for him and when he had his own plans, I wanted him to come up with a Plan B. But even though those were my thoughts, I did support my son and I'm so glad that I did. I'm glad I didn't force him to stay in college. I'm glad I gave him room to pursue the path that was his destiny. I relied on the Lord and let God guide him so that Miles could find his course.

That is the lesson — I handed it all over to God and the Lord took care of my son.

It has been a wonderful journey filled with lots of lessons. That is the reason why I wanted to write this book. To share my story and to share the lessons I've learned. I also wanted to offer you encouragement and give you inspiration. So although my story continues and there is so much going on that has been wonderful, this is where I begin to share a few lessons that will be greatly beneficial to you in your journey.

If I can help you avoid just one of the pitfalls I survived, then that will be a good thing. There is no need for you to go through it if I can help you learn through my experiences. There is no need for you to spend hours trying to figure it out if I can help you become more knowledgeable about the culture. As they say, there is no need to reinvent the wheel.

So take in the lessons and then, enjoy your journey, too. Of course, no two journeys will ever be the same, but the lessons will be similar. My hope is that you will trust the process.

PART TWO
MY LESSONS

Chapter 10

The Importance of Parental Support

Support: To bear or hold up, to serve as a foundation for. To endure, especially with patience, submission; tolerate.

For his entire life, Miles has had his own mind and because of that, we haven't always seen eye to eye. I say up, and he says down. I say red, he says white. It could be a challenge sometimes, but it was a challenge that I welcomed because I raised Miles to be that way; I've always wanted him to follow his own mind.

My son was just like me; I really couldn't tell him anything about anything. He was hardheaded and no matter what, he was going to pave his own path and take his own journey.

It was so hard to get him to listen to me, even when I was setting down the rules at home. When Miles was younger and I was at work, I didn't like Miles having kids in the house because I wasn't present; I wasn't there to supervise. It wasn't that I didn't trust him; there were all kinds of liability issues — I just always wanted to be there to make sure everyone was all right at all times.

So Miles knew, *No company in the house when I'm not home!*

However, did Miles listen? I cannot tell you how many times I came home through the front door, while Miles's little friends were running out the back! Issac…..AKA Earl on the Beat today!

Yup, Miles never listened, but you know what? It's because he didn't listen that he is where he is today. When he told me that he wasn't supposed to be at Alabama State University, that he was supposed to be famous, that he was supposed to be rich...my first instinct was to tell him to just stay there and work it out. I wanted to tell him that he could be rich later.

But there came a point where I realized that what Miles wanted to do was bigger than me and my plans for him. Once I said, "Lord, you take the wheel; I can't do this anymore, I give him back to you," I truly did that. I gave Miles to God and then, I believed God and supported my son.

I had to support my son because just as the dictionary defines support, I had to be that foundation for him. I had to be the place where Miles could stand tall and strong so that he could go after his dream. It wasn't always easy, and there were many times when it was scary.

I knew nothing about this music industry and even once things started rolling for Miles, I didn't know what to expect. So like I said, I just hoped and prayed and prayed some more. As his mother, I just wanted to do right by my son. And what I could do best for Miles was to support him.

Being there, staying in his corner allowed me to help guide him in the right direction as he pursued his dream. This was his life; I had to let him live it, but be there for him as his safety net. He had to know his mother had his back, even if I didn't agree.

Parental support is so important in your child's dream because everyone, especially our children, needs that foundation; they need you there to hold them up and build them up. Once your son or daughter knows you're there for them, that will be when they are able to soar.

I had plans for Miles in my mind. God had Miles's destiny in His hands. Clearly what God had for Miles was much bigger and better than anything I could have imagined. So at that point, I had only one job...and that was to support and be there for my son.

Here is the lesson in this: Parents, you need to understand if you don't support your child, more than likely they are going to pursue their dream anyway. They will do it with or without you. So it's best to get on board to guide your child through the process and to help him/her prevent mistakes that could be destructive or life-changing. Be there every step of the way. It's the best thing you can do.

.

Chapter 11

Importance Of A Strong Team

Team: A number of persons associated in some joint action.

No one can accomplish success alone and that is why a team is fundamental. However, it cannot just be any team; you must have a *strong* team in order to be successful. You must have a team where everyone is playing their position well.

While you are the foundation for your son or daughter, the team is the foundation for all of you. The team is the shoulders on which the artist will stand.

Our team consists of Miles, of course, two assistants, a security guard, a manager, a tour manager, the label, our attorney, an accountant and then me. I'm Mom! I manage the managers so everyone is always on the same page and our team can run like a well-oiled machine.

Besides their professional talents, the team will give you moral support; they can hold you up when you feel like falling down. It is the team who will help you soar higher.

So how do you choose a team? Once you have studied and chosen someone based on their professional skills and expertise, the next thing you must consider is that everyone on your team will be working with you in an intimate way. You will be spending hours together, they will know so much of your business, your personal information and in reality, they will be as close to you as family. So these must be people you trust.

Trust is the beginning. And even if you do trust everyone, always remember to get Non-Disclosure Agreements, also known as NDAs. We have everyone sign an NDA because of how close people will be to us in our lives. NDAs are so important for your protection.

After trust, there's an energy I feel that is very

important. I already told you when I met Coach K and "Pee," I felt their energy. I trusted my gut with them and I was right. You have to feel a good vibe, so always trust your instincts about people. You will be looking for competent, honest, loyal people for your team. You want people who will be rooting for everyone to win. Sometimes, that is something that you'll be able to feel, rather than something you will read on a résumé.

I do want to make a note here about one of the most important positions on your team, that is the position of assistant. The title of assistant may not be as glamorous as the others, but assistants are just as important because they will be the organizers of your life. Often, they will be your eyes and your ears and your gate keepers. You have to choose assistants just as wisely as any other position, so don't downplay that. Oh, and make sure you don't choose an assistant (or anyone, for that matter) who has an interest in being in the industry. Someone with an interest, someone who wants to be a rapper or a singer or someone who wants their own label will be distracted from doing their job. Instead of taking care of your business, that person will be on the lookout for opportunities for themselves. That will definitely get in the way.

So choose everyone, including assistants, wisely with the understanding that teamwork truly does make the dream work.

Chapter 12
Finance

Finance: the management of revenues; the conduct or transaction of money matters.

The most important words in the above definition of finance are: the management of revenues. That is what this section is all about...the management of your money.

The bottom line is this — your finances are important. Very important. Actually, very, very, important. (Did I mention that your finances are important?) The reason you're doing all of this is because yes, it's something that your child loves, but it is to make money. Well, I can tell you the money is gonna come faster than you could have ever imagined, but there's the other side, too — it can go faster than you imagine if you're not prepared to receive it. You must be prepared because while the money is great, it can lead to your downfall if not handled and managed properly.

In the beginning, I gave Miles full control of his money, but one thing you have to remember is that in most cases, your children are still very young. They won't know much about money management. So, I'm glad I was there to help Miles navigate through all of this.

The first thing is that *everything* must be documented for tax purposes because taxes are the first thing that can get the artist into big trouble. The government will always get their money. Period. You have to make sure you have everything lined up.

Most of us weren't raised learning good money management skills, but that's fine. That's why there are professionals; a good accountant can take care of all of that. I would recommend finding one who specializes in music entertainment. It's not necessary, but I highly recommend it because music is certainly a specialty.

Like I mentioned before with everyone on your team, you have to be sure, you have to know that the accountant has your best interest at hand because remember some of those horror stories I mentioned earlier in the book? Well, there have been too many accountants who have mismanaged funds of an artist. There have been people who've embezzled money, who've cleaned artists out. Please don't let that be you.

Start first by educating yourself on your potential accountant's credentials. Do your research, then in your interview with the accountant, ask plenty of questions. Find out who he/she has worked with or who he/she has worked with in the past. Ask for references and make sure you check them. Make sure you check several references. (Anyone who doesn't or is not willing to provide references is not the accountant for you!)

Even though your accountant is crucial to your business, always remember this is your money. Never turn over full control to anyone. So follow up with your accountant often; you need to know how much money you have at just about all times.

Once you've chosen a good person, though, use your accountant's expertise; seek his advice on not only saving and investing your money, but on any purchases you may make, especially larger purchases. Your accountant can keep you on track, making sure you can actually afford what you're about to purchase. Just because you have the money in the bank, doesn't mean you can afford it.

Accountants can also provide good financial planning for you. They can advise whether it's best to rent a place to live or buy a home. They can advise whether it's better to lease a car or buy a car. Because your accountant can see the full picture, he can advise you what's best for your situation at any given moment.

I'm really glad to share this section on finance because there is something I wish we'd done early on, but you live and you learn. We had an accountant, but I wish we'd had a bookkeeper as well. A bookkeeper's job is to keep records of financial affairs; they will help you keep your records in order, helping you to keep track of your daily financial picture, showing your income versus your expenditures.

More than generating money, this business will generate so much paperwork for you...lots and lots of paperwork. A bookkeeper will help you keep up with all of those documents. In today's times, it's a bit easier with credit card companies who allow you to download your bill each month. Still, a bookkeeper will keep track of your money constantly. The better grasp you have on your money, the better you will do.

Like I said earlier, this is one of the reasons why I'm writing this book. This was a lesson learned and one I wanted to share. Having been down this road, I want to make sure I can help as many people as possible not make the mistakes we made — so get a bookkeeper.

Finally, don't shortchange yourself; put as much effort into finding the right accountant as you will put into everything else. This is one area where you cannot afford to take a gamble. You have worked hard for the money, you've been given an opportunity that not many people will have. So you have to do all that you can to secure that money bag.

Chapter 13

Legal Representation

Legal: Of or pertaining to the law, connected with the law or its administration.

There is no one member of the team who's more important than any other; you need each part to work together to make the team work. However, I have to say that I am so happy the first person who joined our team was our lawyer, Uwonda Carter-Scott.

I love our choice of legal representation. We are very, very blessed to work with Uwonda for many reasons. From the beginning, she has been a gem in representing our brand. She always made herself available to take my calls and when she couldn't talk to me then, she called right back and was willing to answer any of my questions at any time. She was always on point letting me know that she was on the team, all in for Miles.

That's who you want — someone who's going to be there when you need them and someone who feels the same sense of urgency that you feel.

Even more importantly, however, you want someone who knows their stuff. You want someone who has not only knowledge of the industry, but knowledge of the culture. I say culture because artists today are not the same as artists from just twenty years ago. These days, artists have so many more income opportunities for these young artists and you need an attorney who can advise on the movement of this new generation.

Because of this when it comes to an attorney, you definitely want to work with someone who has experience; you don't want this to be their first rodeo and there are a few reasons for that. First, you want someone who knows how to navigate through this process and who knows the music and industry jargon. If you go to someone with experience in the industry, you won't have to worry about any kind of learning curve for them. That will make everything so much easier for you. You want an expert in the do's and the don'ts of the industry.

Next, an entertainment attorney most likely will have the relationships and the contacts that are so important in this industry. You want someone who has done this before because those relationships can be crucial to growing your brand. Their contacts become your contacts — and remember, teamwork makes the dream work.

Again, like with other members of your team, you want your attorney to be honest and have the highest standards of ethics and integrity. This is where your research will come into play. You know all lawyers are not good lawyers. Most of them will have reputations (good or bad) that proceed them, so call around. Someone will be able to recommend an attorney and even then, still check out their references.

I suggest that you interview at least three potential attorneys. Show up to the meetings with lots of questions; there should be nothing you're not able to ask. After you have checked out their references, go with the one who gels with you.

All of this is so important because an attorney is negotiating on your behalf, trying to get the most money possible for you. They can make or break a deal; they can make or break a career.

Uwonda and I have become personal friends, though she still handles her business. She has to because she knows when she helps us to win, she wins, too. This has been an amazing professional and personal relationship and it's the kind of relationship that I want for you.

Chapter 14
Deal Making

Deal: To take action with respect to the thing or person. To trade or do business with; a business transaction, an arrangement for mutual advantage.

Now of course, much of the 'deal making' will be handled by your attorney, but it is important for you to be aware of every facet of your child's business. Trust me, there will be a lot of deal making in this industry. From the initial recording contract to endorsements, to even touring, there are always deals being made.

As I said, we were blessed with Uwonda Carter-Scott, but even she encouraged me to stay involved and aware of everything with my son's career because there are constantly deals being made. There are good deals and some not-so-good deals and to protect yourself, no matter what deal you're handling at the moment, every single one should be put in the form of a contract.

I'm telling you that you will meet some wonderful people who will want to make deals on a handshake, but you should never do that. Never do a deal based on a verbal agreement alone. You cannot collect a check on a verbal agreement. Everything must be in writing to protect you and your brand, and to make sure everyone is on the same page in this particular deal.

There may be an instance when you are offered a contract before you have legal representation. I would never recommend signing anything without an attorney. It may be difficult if you feel like you're being pressured and you're sure what's in front of you is a good deal. However, remember those horror stories? So many of them were because of a lack of good legal representation. You don't want to find yourself in a situation where you will have to fight your way out of hell. There are artists who've had to fight for decades to get out of bad contracts, artists who've had to completely change their career while trying to end a bad contract. For example: The Artist Formally Known As.

If you are ever presented with a contract and then find yourself being pressured or rushed to sign that contract, STOP! That's a red flag. There must be some reason why that person doesn't want you to have legal representation. No one should feel pressured to do anything for anyone at anytime.

I cannot say it enough — you want to understand everything in your contract and you can only do that with an attorney. Believe me, it will be in the best interest of you and your brand. This is one place where you will thank me later.

Chapter 15
Avoid the pitfalls

Pitfall: A lightly covered and unnoticeable pit prepared as a trap; any trap or danger for the unwary.

In this industry there are so many pitfalls, so many opportunities to make mistakes. Just like in life, you will find yourself making a few; you won't be able to avoid that. But if you're aware, you can avoid as many of them as possible.

One of the biggest pitfalls can happen when you're team building. We already talked about building the best team that you can, but there will be a temptation to include your friends and family in every position.

Now, putting friends and family in these positions can be great IF they have the experience, if they are truly qualified. The challenge becomes when they are not experienced and they are not qualified. I promise you, if you put in someone who is not equipped to handle the job, it will affect the entire team. You don't want to have any weak links.

So as hard as it's going to be, you have to approach this business professionally. You have to keep feelings and emotions out of the equation because this is your brand and the decisions you make in the beginning will have long lasting effects. It will be difficult to turn some friends or family members down who want to go along for the ride. However, in the end, it will be best for all of you, particularly, it will be best for your son or daughter.

And I have to add this — you cannot allow friends and family to come to you and just mooch. However, you *can* create positions and opportunities so they can eat as well. Listen, your family and friends have to earn a living, I get that. They can either earn a living with your brand or someone else's, and I get that, too. I know everyone needs to earn a living to feed their family. So, if you're going to give them a position to feed them, just make sure it's a position they are qualified to handle. That's for everyone's benefit.

Chapter 16
Touring / The Road

Tour: A traveling from place to place; a long journey visiting a number of places in sequence, especially in an organized manner. A journey from town to town to fulfill engagements.

Touring will be a very exciting part of your child's career and it can also be a very profitable part as well, though there will be times when profit shouldn't be your concern. This is another place where God has blessed us; Ron Byrd is our Tour Manager.

Ron came to us with lots of tour experience and that was exactly what we needed. He'd had the pleasure of touring with acts from Rick James to my son, Lil Yachty, and everyone in between. With the line-up that he's had, he's experienced it all so there was nothing that would surprise him on the road.

What's been great about having someone like Ron is that he has helped me to learn what to expect and what not to expect on the road with a young artist. If you're like me, you will be new to all of this and that's why the expertise of your team is so important. Ron knows it all, so he's taught me what is and what is not part of the culture. He's taught me what is part of the business and the things that I should not accept. He is a wealth of information, has tons of knowledge and he's an excellent teacher who is willing to share it all.

You will find that tours are a lot like relationships. They get better over time if they're planned properly. There are so many moving parts, starting with where your act falls on a tour. This is something that can change on every tour. You can be the opening act, or you can be one of the acts. Then, there's the spot where every young artist hopes to be: the headliner. It just depends on all of the variables that go into the tour.

Let me go through a few of those variables. Touring is really 100 percent about logistics. It all has to make sense, so when touring, you need to partner with a knowledgeable travel agent; someone who will be able to help you with travel and lodging. And someone who can tell you whether air travel is the best way because sometimes ground is better.

You need someone who is going to help you factor in all costs or else you may find yourself going into the red when that isn't necessary. It is definitely possible to do a tour and exceed your budget, but that's not what you got into this business to do.

One thing that's important for me to note as I did in the beginning, touring isn't always about making a profit every time. I was shocked to discover this, but sometimes you will take the loss for money you will earn later. Sometimes, the most important thing is exposure. The key is to know your objective before you begin your touring plan. And then, plan your tour accordingly.

Ultimately, of course, everyone's goal is to headline their own tour, but it's important to be patient and just like every other career, take this step by step; trust the process.

Every act has to start somewhere and like everything in life, many times, that somewhere is at the bottom. It may seem like you're at the bottom, but just remember this is where you start before you can get to the top.

Chapter 17
Merchandising

Merchandising: The planning and promotion of sales by presenting a product to the right market at the proper time, by carrying out organized, skillful advertising, attractive displays, etc.

Merchandising will become another important part of your brand and your business. It will be another profit center for you. Merchandising goes hand in hand with touring, of course, but you can sell your merchandise on tour and in other ways.

Merchandising can be done in-house, which is what I thought I wanted to do at the beginning of Miles's career. I wanted to own all of our merchandise and this way, 100 percent of the profit would come back into our business.

But since all of this was new to all of us, I decided to get the advice of someone who would know. I went to Coach K and told him that I was interested in doing our merchandising.

Right away Coach said, "Are you sure? It's a lot of work, Venita. I don't know that you really want to take on that risk, especially not now. Not when you're learning everything."

So being new in the game, I fell back and we cut a merchandising deal with a very large merchandising company. The contract said that the company was to show up at our events, sell the merchandise and then give us a report at the end. Coach K was right; for us, in the beginning, this was the way to do it.

However, just because we chose to do it this way, this is not the only way that it can be done.

There are lots of artists who control the sales of their merchandise 100 percent. When you handle your own merchandising, you basically create another stream of income. Not only that, this is a place where you can create jobs for family and friends. Just keep in mind that this position, requires working with people you *completely* trust because when you do your own merchandising, you're working with lots and lots of cash. So you must have a merchandising team in your company who is going to be accountable. You will definitely want to have your records in order if this is the option you choose.

No matter which way you go, merchandising will be important for you and your brand. There is not a right way nor a wrong way; everyone has to do what's best for them. Just do something and don't leave that merchandising money on the table.

Chapter 18
Social Media

Social Media: Websites and applications that enable users to create and share content or participate in social networking. Online communication that is used by large groups of people to share information and to develop social and professional contacts.

We live in an amazing time! On a daily basis, we can communicate with hundreds of thousands of people all around the world without leaving the comfort of our homes. One of the things that got my son noticed was that he was extremely savvy with social media.

Miles was able to get his music out to people on platforms such as SoundCloud. People who'd never heard his name and had no idea who he was heard his sound, loved it, told other people and his following just continued to grow and grow.

The number of people he reached was incredible. Hundreds of thousands of people heard his music without Miles having to spend a dollar on advertising or promotion. That's why I say social media is amazing.

However, there is the flip side of social media. While it can be used for good, social media can also kill, steal and destroy you if you allow it. There is a reason why social media is often referred to as the devil and there is a reason why you should treat it as such. All I mean by this is that you should use social media for what it's worth. Use it for your benefit, understanding the whole time there is a good, a bad and an ugly about social media.

The good is what happened to Miles. If used correctly, social media can bring rewards beyond measure. It can bring followers and fame and fortune. It's a fact that social media fuels the income for a lot of these young stars today. There are so many who run their entire business from their followers on social media and they have created great wealth, millions even, off of all the different platforms.

So that is the good, but it can quickly turn to the bad if you're not careful with the content that you put out through social media. Your content is your brand; it can make or break you. Bad content can lead to a lot of negative results. You have to remember that once information is out there, it is out there forever for the entire world to see. There is no way for you to make content disappear completely. That is a factor that must be kept in mind with every single thing you post.

Always keep your ultimate goal in mind — if you're moving toward stardom, there are certain things you want to do and other things that you don't want to do. You don't want anything to come back and haunt you later on. You don't want to lose a deal because of something you posted years ago. So you must be thoughtful and careful about everything, always keeping your mind and an eye on the future.

Another thing about content — never put anything out there that's not true, never put out anything that could cause a controversy. It is just not worth it. Not after you've worked so hard to build your brand.

I often have to remind Miles about the content that he puts out. Displaying your talent is good. However, you don't ever want to mock a brand you've done business with or are doing business with now or a business that you could work with in the future.

I thank God Miles has had so much success in the area of endorsements. He's received all of them because of his image; he's seen as a good role model.

Now, we cannot change our past or the things we've done, but we can be in control of our current situation and our current content, especially if one day, you'd like your brand to be attached to mega brands like: Sprite, Nautica, Target, and Reebok. Companies don't want to be associated with drama or negativity. If you notice, whenever a celebrity finds himself/herself in trouble with the law, the very first thing we hear is how he/she is losing their endorsements; the companies pull out and run the other way. They don't want to be attached to negativity at all.

Miles making the Forbes list is due to the income he's generated from his endorsements, along with the music. I know this is not a possibility for everyone, but endorsements are a great way to grow your income and brand without working too hard. Who doesn't want to earn a check for wearing the latest shoe?

There is a lot of money to be made in this industry; you just have to position yourself so that when the opportunity presents itself, you are ready!

My advice in order for you to be ready...THINK! Think about everything you put on social media. Think about the day when you're asked to be a spokesperson for a company, product or service...but then, you lose a million dollar deal because of something you posted years ago. That may not be fair, but it is the reality; it happens every day.

I cannot stress this enough. If you cannot be proud of it, don't post it. If you can't share it with your family and friends and have them be proud, that is a good sign you should stay away. Think, think, think about your future. Be smart and know that your content could one day land you on (or off) the Forbes List. Always remember that.

Chapter 19

Haters & Trolls

Hater: To dislike intensely and passionately. To feel extreme aversion or extreme hostility toward.

Troll: a person who starts quarrels or upsets people on the Internet to distract and sow discord.

I would be lying if I said this industry was all warm and fuzzy. Being the mother of a artist who still had her doubts when her son made the cover of the XXL magazine, I can tell you it wasn't all warm and it certainly wasn't all fuzzy.

When Miles made the cover of XXL as one of the members of the 2016 freshman class of rappers, I knew in my heart that was the real beginning. When this happened, Miles had already signed with Coach K, though this was before his record deal with Quality Control. But once he was on that cover...this was it. I had really raised a rapper for sure!

I had raised a rapper who was doing what no one else was doing. He was the first in his lane with this happy, upbeat, child-like sound. His songs weren't about hos and guns; he was rapping about his reality. His life was great and that's what his songs were about. He'd made that genre popular and others slowly followed.

Then on top of that, Miles had his own look with his bright red hair with beads. When he walked into a room, he really made you wonder and ask, 'who is this kid?'

However, even though everything seemed to be going so well, it was that XXL cover, with Miles on the verge of signing a deal, that I realized two things: not everybody is happy for you and not everyone celebrates someone who is different.

I think it was because Miles took off so fast; the fortune and the fame was unbelievable. This kid made the Forbes list and with all of that, the haters began to rise up. The haters came out of nowhere and came from everywhere. People didn't like my son — for no reason!

And it saddened me the way people came for him. Grown men and women just didn't care and said horrible things. That was when I discovered that the trolls have no filter. It's as if they never had any home training; they don't care about your age or your gender...they come after everyone. They just don't have any respect.

This was something that I just didn't understand. Whether people liked Miles or not, there was one thing everyone had to do — no matter who you were, you had to respect my son. They had to give Miles credit for the way he was out there doing his thing. He'd created a sound that a group of people called fans bought into. These fans loved Lil Yachty.

But the haters and the trolls didn't care about any of that. And once Miles signed his deal with Quality Control, it got worse. That was when the fruit of his labor quickly began to show: the clothes, the cars, the jewelry — and it wasn't all for him! Miles took very good care of his family and friends, wanting everyone he loved to share in his success. But he had earned it. Nothing had been given to Miles. If anyone really looked at Miles honestly, they would see only one thing — that this young man had gone after his dream with a focus that few people had. For that, he should be applauded, not ridiculed.

Yet, they were there — the haters and trolls. These were just people who wouldn't rock with my son for whatever reason. And that is the lesson.

What you have to remember is that there will always be people who will find something wrong with what you're doing. There will always be people who will talk about you just because they have nothing going on in their lives.

But the trolls didn't stop with Miles; the trolls even came for me! Yes, me, his mom. The woman who carried this boy in her womb for nine months. People would DM me and say all kinds of crazy stuff like: You need to stop spending your son's money.

How do they know what money I'm spending? People have said all kinds of disrespectful things like that and then, when I check out that person's page, I always find that they have zero followers and are following sixteen people: TROLL! Oh yes, beware of the IG (and other platform) trolls!

Even when folks come for me, I never clap back. I

have way too much class, and on top of that, I know doing that is not worth my time, energy or focus. Not when I'm out here trying to support my son and all the moves he's making.

Another reason I don't engage with these people is that I understand I'm not the only one. I am now a good friend with the mother of a Florida rapper, who was murdered and she shared with me that even though her son is no longer with us, she still has to deal with trolls.

I was really taken aback when she told me that. It is unbelievable that even after she had to bury her son, she couldn't bury the direct messages that still came to her saying mean things about her son! Who does that?

It really makes me wonder who are these people? Who raised them?

I know having to deal with all of this is just part of the industry. In today's times, it's part of life, really, and you have to determine how you want to deal with these kinds of things. I would recommend not engaging, not entertaining these people at all. The haters and the trolls come after you because they have no life, but you do. They don't have much positivity going on, but you do. So to me, it's best not to acknowledge them. Don't give them what they want, stay focused on your positivity, on your success because there is nothing you can do about their lives, but there is a lot that you can do about yours.

You may find yourself in situations, though, where you will come face-to-face with someone who has a negative opinion and you have the opportunity to change someone's mind. Sometime ago, I was in a store shopping and the sales rep and I started a conversation. She asked me a couple of questions and it came up that Lil Yachty was my son.

She said, "Really, that's *your* son?"

I could tell by her tone she had a hard time looking at me and making that connection. "Yes, he is," I said. Then, I went on to share with her how awesome he was and how good he'd been to not only me, but to others around him.

She looked at me as if she were stunned. Finally, she said, "Wow! I thought he was from the streets. Maybe it's the red hair; I don't know."

What? She'd deduced all of that just by looking at the color of my son's hair? I couldn't believe it and I just wanted to make sure she understood who my son really was.

Simply because I'm his mother, I will always protect my son. I want to shield him from all things bad, all the things that people are saying. That's only natural, of course, and in this industry, unfortunately as parents or guardians, you're going to have to do a whole lot of shielding, but you can never protect them enough. The haters and the trollers are going to be there and they will take their shots. There's nothing you can do about that. This is just one of the ways the industry will bring some bumps and bruises. All you can do is put your thick skin on, and teach your child to do that same thing.

I'd be lying, though, if I said I was never affected by any of it. From the ugly tweets to the unnecessary beefs to the words that people throw at you can hurt. You'll be faced with lies, rumors and disrespect. Then, you will have to deal with the disappointments and letdowns. And don't forget about the hard feelings because on this journey you will hurt someone you never meant to hurt.

It can be a lonely space because there are not many people who are going through what you're going through. There are not many people who will be able to understand.

Just know you will be able to get through all of it. As long as you remember your self worth and your child's self worth, there is nothing anyone can *say* to bring you down. Your only job is to keep your eye on your prize. Stay focused on the goals you want to achieve; press forward and press through no matter what is going on around you. Just believe in you, believe in your vision because if you don't believe in you, no one else will.

So the bottom line — ignore the haters and the trolls. What they have to say really has nothing to do with you. That's their opinion and they don't know your dreams, they don't know the price you've paid, they don't know your journey.

So you just stay your course!

Chapter 20

Security

Security: freedom from danger, risk. Being safe. Something that secures or makes safe, protection, defense.

Security is an area that has to be taken very seriously. A lot of times when these young entertainers become famous, they forget (or just don't know) what adequate security really is. When they think of security, the first thing that comes to their minds is: I need to hire my big friend.

Well, just because your friend played football at Notre Dame and he could have tried out for the NFL, does not make him qualified to guard your life. He might even be willing to take a bullet for you.

However, that still may not be enough. You don't want any Joe Blow in charge of keeping you safe because this is a serious business. Fans can really get out of control, especially with a popular artist. The more famous the artist, the more security you will need to employ.

Being famous means needing protection. Period. You need smart protection, good protection. Good security is all about being smart, not just big. In fact, what I've found is that you don't have to be big to be good security. The opposite is true, too. Just because someone is big, doesn't make him good at security.

First of all, if someone is going to be your security detail, they need to be able to travel everywhere. You don't want to hire someone only to find out later that he/she has child support issues and can't leave the state. That could be a huge problem if you're heading out on tour in two days.

Also, before you hire security, make sure he/she can be issued a passport and visa. There are countries that will not let someone who's a convicted felon enter. That was one of those on-the-job things that I discovered. I didn't know that and didn't find out until we ran into that situation.

A license to carry a gun is another issue. Whether your security is a man or a woman, everyone must have the proper permits. This is a huge concern because as a performer, you'll be moving between all fifty states and Canada on the regular and your security has to be permitted to carry everywhere.

Then there's the question of carrying a weapon into the airport. There are policies and procedures that you must follow if you're traveling with a weapon. Your security will need to report to the airport hours before your flight leaves to check in their weapons. This was something that I was not aware of.

Safety is the number one concern for your security detail. Your security will be responsible for checking out the venue before your artist enters the building. Security is the one who has to determine and plan any "escape" route; he has to know where all the exits are in case of a fire or anything else. (And while he's at it, make sure he checks out the restroom locations, too.) Security must do everything to protect his client.

The key to all of that is to remember that security is not a game and should not be handled as such. I never handled it as a game, but in the beginning, I hired guys who were not properly trained. (They were big, though!)

After two hires, I realized we had to get trained security to come in and really do the job. We finally hired a retired police officer from the Atlanta police department. It was a smart hire: he had lots of years of protecting the city of Atlanta that he was able to do because of the high levels of rigorous security training he had to go through to have that job.

Take the time to research and evaluate the credentials of your security detail because your artist, your child's life, will be in his or her hands.

Chapter 21
Discipline

Discipline: Activity, exercise, or regimen that develops or improves on a skill, training.

It is very important that you have some level of discipline when you take on this role. This is what you have to remember: T*o whom much is given, much is expected.* As fast as this opportunity has been presented to you, it can be taken away, too. So the best thing for you to do is seize the moment, take care of business and do what you came to do!

When everything started happening for Miles, I'd hoped that I'd done my duties and fulfilled my responsibilities as a parent. I'd hoped I'd taught him how to behave, taught him how to treat others well. I didn't teach him much about business, but I did lead by example, making sure I always handled my business properly. I made sure he saw how I always showed up on time, how I was always present and always properly dressed for every occasion.

I learned that kind of discipline from my parents. My dad did not play; he was an ex-Marine and so, he had my brother and I in check. My dad didn't even have to speak when we were kids. All he had to do was give us the eye and that look would stop us cold and shut us down. We'd see that look and straighten up real quick. Not only did my father have that look, but he also had his rules: no touching anything when we were in the store, no asking for anything in the store, we spoke when we were spoken to.

Those were just a few of the rules and when my father told us that, he meant it. There was no repeating, no second chances when my father spoke. He said what he had to say and his words were the law. My father was a father; he was the one in charge, the head of our household, no jokes.

He didn't believe in sparing the rod and spoiling the child. He was guided by the biblical principle when it came to this kind of discipline. One time, I'd done something that I can't even remember now. But, I got one of those good old-fashioned whoopings.

Afterward, as I cried and cried, I shouted out, "I hate you!" to my father. I couldn't believe I'd said that; it just came out of me.

But all my father said to me was, "Good! Now get in that room before you get some more of what you just got!"

He wasn't fazed at all by my words and didn't have to tell me to go to my room twice. I took my butt into my bedroom, laid down on my bed and took one of those good naps...you know the ones. The nap you take after you just got your butt tore out the frame. That really is some of the best sleep ever!

Here's the thing, though — whenever my parents took me and my brother to an event, people would always comment on how disciplined and well-behaved we were. It was because of the way we'd been raised; my parents had raised us right.

The discipline, however went beyond just the way we behaved. In high school, I learned how to drive and my mom used to let me drive her brand new bright orange Chevette. When I was in that car, you couldn't tell me nothing, but there came a time when I wanted my own car. So, I asked my dad for a car.

His response: "What do you need a car for?"

I did get a car, but needless to say, I bought it myself. (Side note: today my son has eight cars. My, how times have changed.) That was just how my dad was. He didn't give too much; he made us earn everything the way he earned what he wanted. My dad worked hard all day, every day and he wanted us to do the same thing. So much so that when I graduated from high school, my father thought it was time for me to go to work.

While my mother wanted me to attend college, my father thought a job was more in order. A job with good benefits. He thought the steel mill could be just the place. It was where he'd earned a living for thirty-something years. And if I didn't want to be there, he thought the post office was another great option. That was the vision my dad had because that was what he knew. He worked hard and because of his labor we had a nice house, both of my parents had nice cars, there was always food on the table and the lights and cable were never off. So he believed that if he could have a "good life" that way, I could, too.

But I told my father, "No thanks. I'm not interested." I had so many dreams outside of the dreary midwest. There was so much I wanted to do beyond the steel mill. I was going to college, one way or another, with or without his help. I was able to do it, too. I was able to go to college and graduate because of the discipline I'd been taught by my parents.

What I learned from them, I was able to pass to my children. I can be firm with my son and daughter, not as firm as my dad was with us, but enough for my children to respect me and know when I mean business.

This is another reason for Miles's success. He watched, he learned, he listened, most of the time, thank God. He wasn't a perfect child, of course. I've already mentioned how Miles could be stubborn like me and because of that, we did butt heads. However, he listened to and accepted my advice most of the time. Now, he shows up on time, he's present in meetings and he's always ready to work. I couldn't be more proud, especially when people, including industry executives, tell me how much they enjoy working with Miles.

This is a tribute to my parents who taught me and I passed the lessons down. In this industry, you have to walk in the door with discipline because you have to plan to make this work. If you fail to plan, then you plan to fail. Always have a plan no matter where you are in your career. That is what will keep you on task.

Be as professional as you can be; if you don't know something, find someone who does. Explore every option available to you as an artist because remember, you will get out of this life what you pour into it.

Being disciplined is just doing what you need to do when it needs to be done. It's doing what you need to do when there are other things you'd rather be doing. But when you're disciplined, it will pay off in the long run. Trust!

My Advice to the Artists...

If there is one thing I know, it's that you want this badly. You want the fans, the fame, the fortune. You want it all.

My advice to you is to find some patience. Being patient means to quietly and steadily persevere. To bear provocation, annoyance, misfortune, pain, etc. without complaint, loss of temper, irritation or the like. To me, patience means all of that, but it means staying the course no matter what.

Your success can happen overnight. Or it can take years. Either way, you have to stay true to what you believe, true to what's in your heart. No matter what it looks like, no matter what others think, no matter how many IG followers you have. You even have to stay true to you no matter what your mom or dad says — of course, without being disobedient to them.

Even if you find yourself homeless (remember Miles's friend, Perry?) you have to stay the course, keeping your eyes on the prize. You have to believe: 'It's gonna happen for me one day.' Believe that because your day is coming.

Whenever your time comes, though, you want to be prepared for the opportunity. So while you're being patient, continue to hone your craft, continue to practice. Even if you don't have the money to go into a studio and record, you keep practicing, you keep writing, you keep recording those beats. At the same time, educate yourself. Educate yourself on the industry. Do research on things pertaining to music; look up 360 deal and what that means. You want to know what you're getting yourself into before it even happens.

Whatever dream you have you must know that it's on its way. I think you have to believe this in your heart because it's important to put positive energy into the atmosphere. I believe that what you put out is what will come back to you. So stay positive and keep positive people around you.

Now, don't be upset if Mom or Dad can't see your

dream the way you do. Don't be upset if they are not feeling your dream just yet. They will in due time. Just keep grinding, just be patient.

Now, when the time comes, have all of your ducks in a row. Don't sign any paperwork on your own no matter what anyone tells you. Signing on your own is always a bad idea, trust that. Moving ahead without legal representation will most likely land you in trouble that may take years for you to fix.

Like I've said earlier in the book, a lawyer is the best person to look over contracts and other paperwork. You can always contact an attorney and ask if he or she can work on a contingency, meaning that if you sign a deal, they can be paid then. How the attorney will be paid is a conversation that you will have before you hire the lawyer.

While the attorney will handle the paperwork, you will have to handle the relationship when you sign a deal with a label. I suggest that you not accept gifts or favors from labels, or anyone unless you are absolutely sure as to what the gifts mean; why are the gifts being offered? Again, you don't want to be making any agreements you're not aware of or anything that can hurt you down the line.

However, the best piece of advice I can give you is don't allow anyone to rush you into anything. Trust your instincts, get advice, ask questions, but never allow anyone to rush you. Don't be afraid to say, "Can I have twenty-four or forty-eight hours to think about it?"

This is so important. You can't rush the process. You must trust the process. And again, I will say...be patient! Life is going to be what it's going to be and I have a great example to share with you.

When I graduated from high school in 1986, there were two things I knew. One was — I was gonna be a member of Alpha Kappa Alpha Sorority, Inc. and the second thing was — I would one day own a Range Rover. That was my absolute dream car; there could be no substitutes.

Well, after graduation from college (and yes, I became a member of Alpha Kappa Alpha Sorority, Inc.) and after I finished a year in graduate school in Minnesota, I moved to Atlanta to start my life as a grown-up. I started working, earning money and I said to myself, "I think it's about time to go cop that Range."

So one Saturday, I set off to the dealership to get

my dream car. I was so excited as I filled out the application and waited for the salesman to ask me what color I wanted.

Well, that wasn't exactly what he said to me. He told me to come back another day because it wasn't gonna happen this day!

I couldn't believe it. Why couldn't I get this truck? I had a job, I could pay. But finally, I accepted that it wasn't going to happen today. It didn't matter; one day, I would get my dream car. It was coming for sure.

All I needed to be was patient!

Then a few years later, I had an even better job. This time, not only did I have good income, but I made sure that my credit score was where it needed to be. This time, I was good! Good! Do you hear me?

Once again, I made my way to the dealership ready to get my car. I spoke to the salesman, filled out the paperwork, waited to pick out my color and the salesman came back and told me, "Not today, honey."

Wait! What? I had dotted my i's, I had crossed my t's. What was the problem? Where had I gone wrong?

But like last time, I wasn't going to get frustrated. I was going to keep on keeping on. I knew it was bound to happen one day, sooner or later. I just hoped that it would be the sooner rather than the later.

Well, the next time I went to the dealership to buy my Range Rover, there was no paperwork to fill out. Because when the salesman was about to give me the paperwork and ask if I'd be needing their financing, I told him no. I didn't need their financing because I would be paying all CASH.

You see, through this whole process, I was patient. I got a little frustrated, but never for too long. I just continued to do what I was supposed to do when I was supposed to do it. I knew it was going to happen one day, I just didn't know it would be my son who would buy it for me.

This is why I say be patient and trust the process. In spite of all the obstacles that may come your way, believe in your dreams.

I know there will be times when you'll feel like giving up, but you cannot do that. Keep pushing toward that prize. Always keep the prize in mind.

If it happened for Lil Yachty, trust...it can happen for you, too. We are living witnesses that dreams do come true if you believe. There were no shenanigans, there was no hocus pocus, no Illuminati — none of that stuff. It was just pure blessings for which I will be forever grateful.

My Advice to Parents and Guardians…

Just let go! That's the best piece of advice I can give to you as the parent or guardian of a child who wants to pursue his or her dream. If your child displays an interest in a particular area that could be a career, I say by all means, support your son or daughter. It doesn't matter if it's rapping, gaming, skate boarding, modeling, blogging, fashion designing, dancing, or playing any sport — support, support, support!

Now of course, if your child is currently in school, I'm not suggesting dropping out. Not at all. Not unless they have a legitimate and firm deal on the table. Other than that, I truly believe it is best to finish high school. That's just my opinion.

Now, college is a different story. I can say that because of what I know now: College will always be there for your child to explore. But if college is not where they're supposed to be, you have to let your child spread his or her wings. Children need our support. Your child will need support as well as your knowledge, your prayers and your advice on this journey.

I can tell you upfront that this is not going to be easy. If you push back and choose not to support, you will be pushing them out there to make decisions, bad decisions on their own. That is something you don't want to do. It could end up costing a lot later, especially in legal fees.

Just stay in your child's ear about the people they are talking to. And make sure you do your own homework. Social media and the Internet will become your best friend. Google it! Google him! Google her! Google everyone and everything! Everything that you want to know is out there.

So even if you can't quite see their dream, be there for them. Help your child make a plan and then help them follow through and execute that plan. I always told Miles and Nina, "If you fail to plan, you plan to fail!" A plan will keep your child focused and a plan will keep you all on the same page.

This kind of journey can be tough, so constantly remind your son or daughter of the prize. Keep them focused on their craft and encourage them to continue to get better at it. Help them design a plan that will take them to the next level.

Then, because you are their guiding light, make sure *you* stay on track. Here are some things that I believe will help you:

- Beware of the not-so-nice people in this industry. That is just part of it. There are all kinds of people.

- Do your homework. Again...use the Internet, use social media to find out what you don't know.

- Don't pay for anything unless you are clear on what you're paying for. There are all kinds of people who will try to take advantage of you.

- Ask questions! Just like we always tell our children, there is never a dumb question. What is dumb is not asking when there's something you need to know.

- Don't go spending your 401K or life savings just because Johnny wants to be a rock star. Be supportive, but be cautious, especially when it comes to your money.

- Research before you decide who you want on your team and then only choose the best folks. This is important because the team will help you soar. So as soon as you see that your child is serious, get that team together.

- Don't lie to your child. Voice your opinion, but then make sure they know you have their back. Let your child know that he or she has you as their support system. That way, your child will be sure to include you in all that is going on.

- Just like I said in my advice to the artist, I will tell you the same thing — don't sign anything. Don't let your child sign anything without you first taking a look. And then, don't you sign anything without having an attorney give you advice.

- Remember to be patient; this stardom doesn't happen overnight.
- Prep your child for what's to come with stardom. There is the good, the bad and the ugly in this industry just like with everything else in life.
- Remember all money is not good money.
- And lastly, stay encouraging, even if you're not fully on board. Your child needs you.

Just know that none of this will be easy; however, it can be very rewarding. From the beginning, you and your child should decide what role you will play. Then, you delegate other roles to people you trust.

Good luck as you take this journey. I will always make myself and my team available to assist you in any way that I can. You can always keep up with where I'll be and how I can be a resource through my podcast *Raising a Rapper.*

I'm very excited about this venture because I will

be speaking with parents who will share their testimonies of their experiences, their stories of success, and you will even hear about some of the tragic situations of the rise and fall in this industry.

When the going gets tough and it seems as if it's just not happening soon enough, remember if it happened for Lil Yachty, then it can happen for your child, too. Just be patient and trust the process.

Blessings to you,

Lil Yachty's Mom

www.raisingarapper.com

Lil Yachty Bio

A native of Atlanta, Georgia, rap star, singer, songwriter and artist, Lil Yachty is one of biggest artists to emerge on the music scene in years. He first came to prominence with his single "1Night," which has received over 39 million plays on SoundCloud and was certified Platinum by the Recording Industry Association of America.

Since that time, Lil Yachty has exploded in the industry. With almost 9 million IG followers, another 4.8 million on Twitter and 637,000 on Facebook, Lil Yachty is a prominent voice of his generation.

Lil Yachty Music

- Release of "1Night," August, 2015
- Debut Mixed Tape, Lil Boat April, 2016
- Signed Joint Venture Deal with Quality Control Music and Capitol Records, June, 2016
- Released second mixtape: "Summer Songs 2," July, 2016
- Debut studio album, "Teenage Emotions," May 2017
- Released Sophomore Album, "Lil Boat 2," March, 2018
- Released: "Nuthin' 2 Prove," October, 2018

TV appearances

- Jimmy Kimmel
- Good Morning America

- Wild N Out
- Snoop and Martha
- The Talk
- Fear Factor
- George Lopez
- MTV Trl

Films

- MTV: "How High 2"
- "Long Shot"
- "Life-Size 2: A Christmas Eve"
- "Teen Titans Go To The Movies"

Brand Space

- Appeared in Yeezy Fashion Show Season 3
- Sprite commercial with LeBron James,
- Nautica

- AXE
- TikTok
- Reebok
- Pink Dolphin
- Chef Boiardi
- Target
- Disney Beats
- Puma
- Tobacco free campaign
- Jeremy Scott/Uggs
- Bape, Collab Collection of Tees and Hoodies.

Press

- *Fader,* Summer Music Issue, July/August 2017
- *Paper,* Summer 2017
- *Rolling Stone,* Lil Yachty's 'Teenage Emotions' Might Change the Way People Rap

- New York Times, Men's Style, The Rapid Rise of the Rapper and Style Star Lil Yachty, December, 2016
- *New York Times Magazine*, 25 Songs That Tell Us Where Music is Going,
- New York Times, Music Section, The Best...of the Grammys, February, 2017
- *The New Yorker,* What Lil Yachty's Optimism Means, May, 2017
- *GQ,* We Should All Be Lil Yachty,
- *Esquire,* Best Dressed Men of the 2017 Grammy Awards,
- *Vogue,* The Best Met Gala Street Style
- Target Ad (aired first during the Grammys) It Takes Two with Carly Rae
- *Rolling Stone*, The Hot List, Hot Rebel MC Lil Yachty
- Billboard, Lil Yachty, Raps Next Big Thing on his Unapologetic Approach to Hip-Hop

- MTV News, Is Atlanta's King of the Teens Destroying Hip-Hop or Just Creating a New Playground For His Friends and Followers?
- The Village Voice, Hip-Hop Hall Monitors, October, 2016
- Complex 50 Best Albums #31 Lil Yachty, Lil Boat
- Noisey, The 100 Best Albums of 2016, #16 Lil Boat
- *Forbes* 30 Under 30 Music, 2017
- Complex, Lil Yachty and LeBron James Shine in Their Hilarious New Sprite Commercial
- Noisey, Lil Yachty's Bubblegum Trap Is Sailing the Rap Internet's Uncharted Waters
- *New York Magazine,* August, 2016
- *XXL*, The 9th Annual Freshman issue, June, 2016
- *XXL,* The Powers That Be, Spring, 2017
- Nautica campaign ~~for~~ Urban Outfitters,

- *XXL,* Lil Yachty Goes Sailing with XXL, August, 2016
- *Fader,* Lil Yachty Discuss His Upcoming Teenage Emotions With Snoop Dogg
- *Esquire,* The 18-Year-Old Prodigy Is the Future of Hip-Hop
- Noisey, Nardwuar Talked to Lil Yachty About Childhood and Coldplay and There Was Much Rejoicing, August, 2016
- MTV News, Lil Yachty Earns His Title as King of Teens, July, 2016
- Interview Magazine, July 2016
- W, About that Yacht Life: How Teen Rapper Lil Yachty Made It Big, May, 2016
- *Playboy,* Teen Atlanta Rapper Lil Yachty on the Stifling Internet Rapper Stigma, March, 2016
- Respect, Lil Yachty's New Mixtape 'Summer Songs 2' July, 2016

- Mass Appeal, Time Alone with Lil Yachty, May, 2016
- Mass Appeal, Up Close & Personal: Lil Yachty & Coach K, April, 2016
- *The Source,* Lil Yachty, Yung Jake and Sonny Digital Provide An Artistic Statement At the MOMA, May, 2016
- VMan, Lil Yachty, the Atlanta Rapper Making Waves

Awards

Billboard Music Awards, 2017, Nominations:

- Top Rap Collaboration
- Top Rap Song
- Top Streaming Song (Audio)

MTV Video Music Awards, 2017, Nominations:

- Best Hip Hop Video
- Best Collaboration

- Best Visual Effects

Grammy Awards, 2017, Nomination:

- Best Rap/Sung Collaboration

HeartRadio Much Music Video Awards, 2017, Nomination:

- Best New International Artist

MTV Europe Music Awards, 2017, Nomination:

- Best Video

Printed in Great Britain
by Amazon

26139736R00098